Prov 3:9-10
Acts 20:35
Giving: Prov 22:9 *Lk 1:37,*
2 Cor 9:6 *18:27*
p.56 Luke 6:46 *Deut 8:17-18* *Neh 8:10*
Lk 19:41 *2 Cor 12:9* *1 Sam 2:30*

Tithes of Honor

...Tithing Under the Order of Melchizedek!

1 Sam 15:22-23 *Matt. 25:23 p79*
Eccl 11:2-6 *2 Cor 8:12*
1 Sam 2:8

p.93 unending manifestation of deliverance
p.95 & revelation
p.96 Hebrews 7:4
p.97 p.99 Act 19:18-20
p.98, 102, 109 p.120

(Formerly, *Tithing Under the Order of Melchizedek*)

By

FRANCIS MYLES

Tithes of Honor: Tithing Under the Order of Melchizedek

Published by:

Francis Myles International
1776 N Scottsdale Rd,
Suite 2467
Scottsdale, AZ 85252
www.francismyles.com

Cover Design by
Carmela Real Myles

Distributed globally by Createspace an Amazon Company

Author's Hall of Appreciation

The Lord gave the word: great was the company of those that published it. Psalm 68:11

It has been said that great projects are never the work of one man, but the collective effort of a team that shares a common destiny. I want to give a heartfelt God bless you to the following brothers and sisters for making the publishing of this book a reality. May God give you a tremendous harvest for every person who will be transformed by the truths contained in this book:

- My dear wife Carmela Real Myles, you have already shown me that you are more than what I asked the Lord for.
- Pastor Olakunle Soriyan for believing in the message of this book and opening up the great nation of Nigeria for my ministry
- Apostle Lee and Prophetess April Roberson for being the best example of what consistent tithing looks like. I am proud to be your spiritual father
- To Linda Vega and Karen Hosey, no spiritual father can ever ask for better spiritual daughters, who have lived the spirit of the message of this book
- Thomas and Rose Richburg, thank you for migrating from New York to come and help my wife, and I build the church in Arizona
- To my army very dedicated intercessors, Damarius, Renee, and Susan

- To Jeffrey and Clara Mzwimbi thank you for embracing my message to the Body of Christ whole-heartedly
- To all the faithful members of Lovefest Church in Tempe, Arizona

Dedication

This book is dedicated to:

i. The Kingdom of God that is advancing into every sphere of human enterprise around the world

ii. To Senior Pastors of Churches who are looking for a more excellent way of exacting the tithe from their faithful followers in order to advance the Kingdom of God

iii. To all the Josephs and Daniels, Lydias and Esthers in the Marketplace who have been looking for a more excellent way of tithing

iv. To the all the faithful who have supported the church for centuries through their tithes and offerings

v. To all disfranchised tithers who have ever said, *"Help, my tithing is not working for me!"*

vi. To all those who have said, *"Tithing is not for New Testament believers!"*

vii. To the faithful members of my congregation, "Lovefest Church International" who have chosen to sow their lives into the apostolic vision to transform nations that God has placed on my life.

TABLE OF CONTENTS

Endorsements

There are **several** attacks on the Church having to do with several issues such as structure; separation of Church and state but the most vehement argument of all has to do with the issue of tithing, whether to be or not to be. Dr. Francis Myles has written a truly inspirational, revelational, insightful, biblical expose' regarding tithing. This book is a must read for all who desire the blessing of God in their life.

Dr. John P. Kelly, *Presiding Apostle*-International Coalition of Apostles, *Founder & CEO*-International Christian Wealth Builders Foundation.

Tithing Under the Order of Melchizedek: The Return of the Lost Key, is a revelation from God and it addresses one of the most misunderstood subjects in the Bible, "tithing." In this powerful book, Dr. Francis Myles continues to lead God's people to righteous living by sharing God's wisdom concerning the Order of Melchizedek. I strongly recommend this book for everyone who calls upon the Lord.

Dr. Robert Watkins, Chairman & CEO Kings & Priests International

It is my prayer that every reader of this explosive book will embrace the truth of its message and enter into a NEW WAY OF LIVING. Dr. Myles has once again provided wisdom and insight from above to empower every believer who has decided to move forward in the Kingdom. It is my desire to HONOR DR MYLES as the MAN OF GOD he is with this endorsement. I encourage everyone to add Dr. Francis Myles to their required reading lists and help break the monotony of unfruitful living. To GOD be the GLORY!

— Prophet Jess Bielby, D.D.
President of Gospel Associates Inc., and
President of Best Home Foods Benton, Kansas

After seeing the dire need for the Lord's people to embrace truth regarding the tithe, giving and receiving, sowing and reaping, I had plans to write a book on the subject. This, however, is no longer necessary. The Lord raised up Francis Myles, a more capable servant, whom He has given the inspiration, revelation, interpretation, application, and communication to benefit the body of Christ. These are the closing days of global financial meltdown, socialistic tendencies and spiritual anemia in the body of Christ. We, therefore, must, with the help of this apostolic word on "Tithing under The Order of Melchizedek," graduate from the milky letter of the law, to the meaty spirit of wisdom and revelation. I believe that this word takes the Church from the failing systems of theology to the divine revelation of Kingdom "theonomics" to inherit the full blessing of Abraham.

I recommend this writing to the entire Church throughout the world as an indispensible truth to help bring us to the measure of the stature of the fullness of Christ.

Bishop Robert E. Smith, Sr.
Total Outreach for Christ Ministries, Inc. Little Rock, Arkansas

Foreword

Dr. **Francis Myles** does a masterful job of bringing the whole issue of tithing out of the Old Testament and into New Testament life. Most New Testament believers are still living in Old Testament lives. So often this is the result not because of the activities of our life, but the understanding and spirit from which these activities flow. As you read Tithing Under the Order of Melchizedek: The Return of the Lost Key allow the Holy Spirit to empower you with fresh understanding for a release of faith through the realm of tithing. Understanding grants us access into new faith realms, which in turn embraces new levels of God through our acts of obedience. This book will help you in your journey in the Lord.

Apostle Robert Henderson,
Author: *Operating the Courts of Heaven*
Robert Henderson Ministries, Dallas, Texas

Preface

Why did I write this book?

I wrote this book first and foremost because, after nineteen years of research, the Lord gave me the permission to write the revelation that He gave me to give to the body of Christ concerning the priestly Order of Melchizedek. I wrote this book to hopefully do my part in helping upgrade the "technology of tithing" in the global church and challenge "inaccurate patterns of tithing" which have limited our spiritual inheritance in God's Kingdom economy.

I wrote this book because there is a cry in the heart of God for His church to "rediscover the tithe of Abraham" and become divorced from the contemporary Malachi 3:8-12 pattern of tithing. However, I did not write this book to stop people in the global church from tithing, because there is a High Priest after the Order of Melchizedek, even our Lord Jesus Christ, who receives the endowment of tithe from His blood-washed people, who live under the New Testament.

I wrote this book to reveal "a more excellent way of giving or exacting the tithe" -indeed, a more excellent way that will reveal the mightiness of our God and restore the "Joy of tithing" to multiplied millions in the global Church. When less than thirty percent of members of the body of Christ tithe consistently, we have to admit that something is terribly wrong with our popular methods of exacting the "tithe" from God's people. We cannot simply relegate the remaining seventy to eighty percent of inconsistent or non-tithers to simply being a group of disobedient Christians, without simultaneously questioning the spiritual technology we are employing in our Churches for exacting the tithe.

"To be free is not merely to cast off one's chains, but to live in a way that respects and enhances the freedom of others."
— Nelson Mandela, former President of South Africa

I wrote this book because I wanted to share the freedom and exceeding joy that tithing according to the pattern revealed in this book has brought to my own life and to the life of our Church. True freedom is not a gift that you can hold to yourself, because its "greatest power and expression" is found in sharing it with others. The sharing of the truths contained in this writing has helped increase the tithing percentages of our Church as some of our non-tithing people and those who tithed inconsistently, discovered the "joy and privilege" of tithing into God's Kingdom. All technologies, whether they are natural or spiritual, must first be tested at their point of origin, to make sure that they are both credible and functional. I want you to know that the spiritual technology for a "New Way of Tithing in the Global Church" which is described in this book is credible, functional and above all biblical.

I also wrote this book to give answers to the following people.

✓ Anybody who has ever said, "help; my tithe is not working for me!"
✓ Anybody who has ever asked the question, "how can I tithe from an inspired heart instead of tithing from a regulated heart?"
✓ Anybody who uses the "Malachi 3:8-12 pattern of tithing!"
✓ Anybody who has ever desired to know how Abraham, Isaac and Jacob "tithed and why they tithed!"
✓ Anybody who has ever asked the question, "Is tithing for today?"
✓ Anybody who has "lost the Joy of tithing!"
✓ Spiritual leaders who are looking for a manual to help them establish "a more excellent way of tithing" in their churches.

I also wrote this book to bring apostolic clarity to the following subjects as they relate to the priestly Order of Melchizedek:

✓ The priestly order of Melchizedek and why Abraham tithed into it.

- ✓ The differences between the priestly Order of Aaron and the Order of Melchizedek.
- ✓ The Power of the tithe of Abraham.
- ✓ Abraham's natural and spiritual inheritance.
- ✓ The spiritual benefits of the priestly Order of Melchizedek
- ✓ A more excellent way of tithing and a new way of living.
- ✓ Why Malachi 3:8-12 pattern of tithing is not God's best for New Testament believers.

I know that there might be some of you who may get angry at me for attempting to divorce the global Church from the "popular Malachi 3:8-12 pattern of tithing!" I assure you that I know exactly how you feel because there was a time I would have defended the Malachi 3:8-12 pattern of tithing with my very life; but God has ways of "cornering us and reconfiguring our internal spirit dynamics." I am asking that whether it's out of your own curiosity or out of the maturity of your patience, to simply allow me "my day" in the "courtroom of your mind."

I know that this teaching may challenge some of your long-held views about tithing, whether you believe in tithing or not. If, after reading this book, you still do not see the validity of my arguments, then you are free to dismiss my thoughts, as the thoughts of a misinformed or misguided man. But I am beseeching you by the sure mercies of God to give this book a fair and reasonable "entrance into the courtroom of your mind." It's my heartfelt prayer that this writing will "Upgrade and shift the technology" of your understanding and practice of tithing and introduce you to a more excellent way of Kingdom living.

God's Servant

Dr. Francis Myles
Senior Pastor, Lovefest Church International
Author: *The Order of Melchizedek*

Chapter One

A Question That Changed My Life!

Then Melchizedek king of Salem brought out bread and wine, he was the priest of God Most High. And he blessed him and said: "Blessed be Abram of God Most High, Possessor of heaven and earth; And blessed be God Most High, who has delivered your enemies into your hand." And he gave him a tithe of all.
Genesis 14:18-20

I remember it, like it happened yesterday, even though it's over two decades later. It's the story of my life. It's a story of divine interception and realignment. It's the story of how God arrested me for becoming a global steward of the revelation on the Order of Melchizedek. I was only twenty-two years old when I became a senior pastor of my own church in Lusaka, the capital city of the beautiful landlocked country of Zambia.

In my church, there was a godly old woman that we all affectionately called "mother." In the Zambian culture, any woman of your birth mother's age or above is given the respect of a mother. This woman was an exemplary and godly Christian. No pastor could have asked God for a better church member. She was never involved in any form of church drama. If there was a problem, she was the one fixing it.

One day after I finished preaching on a Sunday service, she stopped to talk to me. "Pastor sorry for bothering you, but I would like to get an appointment to meet with you." She said graciously. I was very blessed by her request for a meeting because she had never asked for one before. I quickly obliged. Unbeknown to me, God had chosen to use this meeting to ambush me with His grace. Looking back now, I realize that the meeting was not for the woman; it was for my benefit and that of millions of followers of Christ across the globe.

The Meeting

When I finally met with the godly woman we affectionately called "mother," we sat across from each other. Her face looked slightly downcast and troubled. I shifted nervously in my seat. "Was she sick?" I wondered. I finally gathered the courage to say, "Mother how can I help you?" "Thank you, pastor, for taking time to meet with me." She declared. "My pastor before I tell you what is troubling me, I want to first give context to my questions, so you know that I am not here to question your teachings or the authority of any man of God. Pastor, I also want you to know that I know that when anything God has promised is not working, its because something is broken on the human side, for God is always right." I swallowed hard as I did not know where she was trying to go, but I listened attentively. However, the seriousness of the moment began to weigh heavily on me.

"Pastor, all of you Pastors say that if we give our tithes, God will open the windows of heaven and pour out such a blessing that they will not be enough room to receive it." Unrestrained tears ran down her face, creating contours around her cheeks. I shifted in my chair nervously. She recovered momentarily, wiped her tears with a stroke of her palm. "Pastor, ever since I discovered that the LORD wanted me to pay my tithes, I have never missed a tithe in at least 20 years. Sometimes tithing for me is the decision between choosing between my tithes and bus fare. During those times I have chosen to retain my tithe money and then just walked 1 hour to church, rather than catch a bus. Pastor, I am just an old woman who would like to see the blessing of the Lord upon my life before I breath my last breathe. Pastor, please help me! Why is my tithe not working for me? Please show me what I am doing wrong." She cried.

కౌ§ాౌ§ాౌ§ాౌ

Unrestrained tears ran down her face,
creating contours around her cheeks.

కౌ§ాౌ§ాౌ§ాౌ

A Noiseless Change!

The unthinkable happened. I was completely speechless, and my mouth became dry. I had to drink some water just to clear my throat, before I gave her my answer. At that moment I had an epiphany. I suddenly realized that I had never really researched the subject of tithing even though I passionately proclaimed the Malachi chapter 3 tithing system. I realized that everything I knew about tithing was "inherited teachings on tithing" by my spiritual fathers in the faith. I simply resold to my congregation what I had been sold about the subject of tithing. When I finally recovered, I gave her the most honest answer I could give her at the time, but the answer I gave her sounded hollow even to me, but I couldn't lie. "Mother, I do not know why your tithing is not working for you, but I not rest until I found out why?" My lips became even drier as I my own ears digested my hollow response to such a fundamental question. Unbeknown to me at the time, I had just been divinely "ambushed by grace." A noiseless change had taken place in my life that would cause me to write books like *The Order of Melchizedek* and the book on tithing that you are reading now. If you had told me then that I would be the author of *The Order of Melchizedek*, I would have told you that you are out of your mind!

"Thank you, Pastor, for your honest and for taking time to hear me." She declared respectfully. She stood up, said her goodbyes and walked away. I will never forget her dejected and hopeless look when it dawned on her that I had no answers to ease her pain. I died a thousand deaths inside. My determination to research the subject of tithing became even more cemented. Later, I met with one of my elders and told him that I could no longer collect tithes in good conscience on Sundays until I could answer the woman's question. I asked him to be the one to collect tithes on Sunday, while I focused on teaching and praying for the sick.

The Answer Comes!

Unfortunately for the woman (mother) the LORD moved me to South Africa from Zambia before I finally got the answer on the subject of tithing from the Lord. My deepest regret is that when the answer finally came, I had lost touch with the woman we had affectionately called "Mother" and she has since relocated to Heaven. I have always told the LORD that when I get to Heaven the first two people I want to see, is the Lord Jesus Christ and then this woman, to whom I now owe that I now know about the glorious and eternal priesthood of Melchizedek.

❦❦❦❦❦❦❦

A noiseless change had taken place in my life that would cause me to write books like The Order of Melchizedek
❦❦❦❦❦❦❦

And the king of Sodom went out to meet him at the Valley of Shaveh (that is, the King's Valley), after his return from the defeat of Chedorlaomer and the kings who were with him. 18 Then Melchizedek king of Salem brought out bread and wine; he was the priest of God Most High. 19 And he blessed him and said: "Blessed be Abram of God Most High, Possessor of heaven and earth; 20 And blessed be God Most High, Who has delivered your enemies into your hand." And he gave him a tithe of all. 21 Now the king of Sodom said to Abram, "Give me the persons, and take the goods for yourself." 22 But Abram said to the king of Sodom, "I have raised my hand to the Lord, God Most High, the Possessor of heaven and earth, 23 that I will take nothing, from a thread to a sandal strap, and that I will not take anything that is yours, lest you should say, 'I have made Abram rich'— Genesis 14:17-23

One day something spectacularly supernatural happened to me that I will never forget for as long as I live. When the answer to the "tithing dilemma" finally came, God put on a show. Suddenly the whole of Genesis chapter fourteen came alive. It was like watching a movie. All the characters in the story became I animated. I saw this mysterious

4

priest called "Melchizedek" offering Abram the covenant meal of communion (bread and wine), and then I saw something I had never seen before! I saw the words, "and Abram gave him tithes of all!" These words were flashing in my mind like red neon lights. Suddenly the Holy Spirit brought the face of the woman (mother) to my remembrance. The Spirit of God said to me, "Son you never answered her question. Why is her tithe not working for her? As a matter of fact, why is not working as it should for thousands of my people around the world?" The Spirit declared. I was stunned. "Could it be that you guys (pastors) are teaching my people to tithe into the wrong priesthood. You are the seed of Abraham, how come Abraham is tithing into a priesthood that you guys (pastors) don't even talk about. Francis, how much do you know about the priesthood of Melchizedek?" The Spirit asked.

"LORD, I don't know anything." I declared. "How would you like Me to teach you about the priesthood of Melchizedek?" The Spirit of God asked me again. "Please teach me." I declared enthusiastically. Unbeknown to me this would lead to over a decade of intense teaching by the Holy Spirit on the unveiling mysteries of the Melchizedek priesthood.

✿✿✿✿✿✿✿

***Could it be that you guys (pastors) are teaching
my people to tithe into the wrong priesthood.***

✿✿✿✿✿✿✿

In 2008 the Holy Spirit finally gave me permission to write my book *The Order of Melchizedek*, followed another book *Tithing Under the Order of Melchizedek*. The second book has since been rewritten for easy reading, producing the book that you are reading now, *Tithes of Honor: Rediscovering Tithing Under the Order of Melchizedek*. It's my heartfelt prayer that the contents of this book will cause you to take another fresh look at this very important kingdom principle of "tithing." I also hope to help senior pastors move away from the "legalistic dictates of the popular Malachi 3 tithing system" for a "more excellent way of tithing that is driven by the engines of grace and faith, instead of the Mosaic Law." It goes without saying that New Testament believers are not under the Law but under Grace (John 1:17). Consequently, they have to be another pathway that perpetuates the kingdom "principle of tithing" under the dispensation of grace instead of wallowing in the muddy waters of legalism. I am convinced that you will never look at tithing the same way again after you finish reading this book.

LIFE APPLICATION SECTION

Point to Ponder:

They are thousands of faithful tithers all over the world, who are wondering why the tithe is not working for them, as it should!

Memory Verse:

But Abram said to the king of Sodom, "I have raised my hand to the Lord, God Most High, the Possessor of heaven and earth, 23 that I will take nothing, from a thread to a sandal strap, and that I will not take anything that is yours, lest you should say, 'I have made Abram rich' — Genesis 14:22-23

Reflections:

1. What did question did the godly woman ask me that I couldn't answer?

_____

_____

_____

_____

2. Does her question ring true in your life or not?

_____

_____

_____

_____

3. Who was the first man in the Bible to give tithes of honor?

_____

_____

_____

_____

Chapter Two

Is Tithing for Today?

Here (on Earth) mortal men receive tithes, but there (in Heaven) he (Jesus) receives them, of whom it is witnessed that he lives. [9] Even Levi, who receives tithes, paid tithes through Abraham, so to speak, [10] for he was still in the loins of his father when Melchizedek met him. Hebrews 7:8-10 (Emphasis by Author)

O ne of the most frequently asked questions in Christendom is a question that is related to the practice of tithing in the global Church. The question frequently asked is: "Is tithing for today?" This seemingly innocent question arouses some of the most passionate debates among the saints, pitting those in favor of the biblical practice of tithing against those who believe that "tithing" is Modern-day extortion of gullible saints by Modern-day Pharisees.

These heartfelt debates over the practice of tithing have only increased with the increase in the economic decline of many nations. These "tithing debates" in the blogosphere have also been fueled to the point of explosion by the "unrestrained and extravagant lifestyles" of many of the notable proponents of the "gospel of prosperity."

I am the senior pastor of a thriving Church in Arizona (Lovefestchurch. com), founder of Marketplace Bible International (marketplacebible. com) and I am also an itinerant minister of the gospel and a serial author. My unique position in the Kingdom of God has given me a "vantage point" to preside over the question, "Is tithing for today?" I had looked into the eyes of many well-meaning Christians (Kingdom citizens is a better description) who told me how their life and personal economy changed for the better when they started tithing. I have also looked into the eyes of very sincere, God-loving children of God who have told me, "Francis, my tithe is not working for me. I have been tithing for years but the windows of heaven I was promised never opened for me." I have also looked into the eyes of those who have told me to my face that they do not believe that tithing is applicable to post- Calvary New Testament believers. Many in this latter group are usually hardcore non-tithers.

ৡৡৡৡৡৡ

The question frequently asked is:
"Is tithing for today?"

ৡৡৡৡৡৡ

Then there are those who believe that only they are best qualified to administer their own tithes, either because they are part of a home church fellowship where there is no formal tithing structure in place, or because they have lost confidence in the stewardship mechanism or leadership of their local church. At this point, my only caution to this group of disillusioned or disenfranchised saints is that there is no Biblical precedent for tithing into oneself. Tithing from its roots and origins, when Melchizedek the King-Priest intercepted Abraham (Genesis 14), is always connected to a legitimate and God-designated priesthood. In Abraham's case, the tithes left his hands and were given into the Order of Melchizedek. The tithes from the spoils that Abram had taken from the four kings who raided Sodom and Gomorrah did not end up in one of his private bank accounts. I will speak more about this in a later chapter.

A Downward Trend

Whatever side of the tithing debate you find yourself on, what is becoming increasingly clear is that there is an unmistakable downward trend regarding the biblical practice of tithing in the global Church and that there is a great division, confusion, ignorance, and controversy surrounding this important subject. Many congregations in the global Church are reporting the lowest levels of tithing in their congregations than probably at any other time in their church history. This serious decline in tithing is far worse in the United States and other developed nations than in most third world nations, at least on a per capita basis. What is interesting is that this global downward trend in tithing is happening at a time when there has been such a "mass proliferation" of the "prosperity message" via Christian television networks. Many pastors of small-sized churches are having to take on secular employment to help supplement their income and support their families, and some of the spouses of these pastors are also having to find secular employment in order to survive financially.

Why the Downward Trend?

I have lived long enough to know that there is always a reason for the madness. God created us and placed us in a universe of "cause and effect." There are many causes and underlying reasons that are masked in the downward trend in tithing in the global church, and we will do well to understand them. Some of the "causes" behind the decline in tithing come in the form of questions on tithing that the Church has failed to answer adequately. Some of the causes of this decline in tithing come in the form of "inaccurate doctrines on tithing" that are spreading like wildfire on the Internet and blogosphere; many of these teachings have some elements of truth in them but are not based upon the "full counsel of God" concerning the practice of tithing in the New Testament.

By far, the biggest culprit behind the serious decline in tithing in the global Church is the "tarnished testimony and unrestrained extravagant lifestyles" of many of the notable prosperity preachers of our time. I want to go on record as saying that I believe that there is a place of true biblical prosperity that God has for His people. I believe that God desires to bless His children with both financial and material resources to advance His kingdom here on earth. Notwithstanding, I also believe that believers who come into a place of "financial and material prosperity" but fail to understand "divine restraint" are a curse to themselves and they can also bring great injury and harm to the cause of Christ. Poverty and Prosperity are two different extremes of the human condition but Jesus spent a lot of His time on earth, as recorded in the Gospels, talking about Stewardship since God is always most interested in the motives and condition of our heart and how well we manage the "little" that He has entrusted to us. According to Scripture, the primary purpose of prosperity is not for ourselves, but for others, and for His Kingdom.

ɩɣɩɣɩɣ

In Abraham's case, the tithes left his hands and
were given into the Order of Melchizedek.

ɩɣɩɣɩɣ

Enter the Blogosphere

For the time will come when they will not endure sound doctrine, but according to their own desires, because they have itching ears, they will heap up for themselves teachers; [4] and they will turn their ears away from the truth, and be turned aside to fables.
2 Timothy 4:3-4

The advent of the Internet, coupled with the incredible power of massive search engines such as Google and Yahoo, has accelerated the mass proliferation of "information" in today's world. While we celebrate the ability to move and amass massive blocks of information in seconds with the mere click of a mouse, this newfound freedom has also come with a serious downside. The downside to amassing and accessing massive blocks of information lies in the fact that information can be very beneficial or toxic. The blogosphere is full of both good and spiritually toxic information, especially on the subject of tithing.

The advent of the Internet also means that pastors can no longer think that they are the only ones who are influencing their people's attitudes towards the biblical practice of tithing. Whether pastors like it or not, many of the people in our churches are going to the Internet and "Googling" for a second opinion on much of what is being taught in the church. I have found that this is especially true when it comes to dealing with the Church's teaching on tithing. Tithing affects the wallets and purses of the people in our congregations, and assuming that some of our people are not "Googling" for a second opinion on such an important subject is a lesson in naiveté on our part. When the Lord told me to write this book, He directed me first to the Bible, and then to the Internet. The Lord challenged me to "Google" the word "Tithing" just to get a feel of what was being discussed on the blogosphere concerning this critical subject. What I discovered was both enlightening and disheartening. Some of the concerns some people on the blogosphere have on the practice of tithing in the global Church are based upon very legitimate concerns that we cannot dismiss lightly.

God is always most interested in the
motives and condition of our heart

Some of the people who expressed their opinion on tithing on the blogosphere were outright hostile, and many of them had very strong opinions against prosperity preachers. Some of the people in the blogosphere provided half-baked teachings on why they believe that tithing is an unscriptural act under the New Testament. Some went as far as calling tithing under the New Testament a sin. I quickly concluded that the blogosphere on tithing that I was on was patronized by three classes of Christians: "Self-appointed teachers, seekers, and rebels." These are the classes of people who patronized this particular blogosphere. I was particularly drawn to many of the sincere seekers on the blog. Most of them were simply looking for a "more excellent way" of approaching the question and practice of tithing. This book is my heartfelt response to people of faith everywhere are sincerely looking for a "more excellent way of tithing."

LIFE APPLICATION SECTION

Point to Ponder:

The unrestrained extravagant and scandalous lifestyles of some proponents of the prosperity gospel is one of the reasons there has been a decline in tithing in the Body of Christ

Memory Verse:

Here (on Earth) mortal men receive tithes, but there (in Heaven) he (Jesus) receives them, of whom it is witnessed that he lives. 9 Even Levi, who receives tithes, paid tithes through Abraham, so to speak, 10 for he was still in the loins of his father when Melchizedek met him. Hebrews 7:8-10

Reflections:

1. Give two reasons why there has such a steep decline in tithing among so many Christians?

_____

_____

_____

_____

2. Why is tithing such a controversial topic in the Body of Christ?

_____

_____

_____

_____

3. Are there questions on tithing that you feel the church has failed to answer? If so list one of them…

_____

_____

_____

_____

Chapter Three

Hardcore Questions on Tithing

So Philip ran to him, and heard him reading the prophet Isaiah, and said, "Do you understand what you are reading?" [31] And he said, "How can I unless someone guides me?" And he asked Philip to come up and sit with him. Acts 8:30-31

While **I was** making my divinely orchestrated visit to the blogosphere, I was touched by a couple of the questions that were posed by some of the self-appointed teachers, seekers, and rebels on the blog. I was touched by many of these questions because they unmasked many of the sentiments about "tithing" that are held by many of the people who patronize our churches. These questions gave me much-needed insight as to why there has been such a serious decline in tithing in the global church. I will list here some of the questions and teachings on tithing that came from the blogosphere that underscore the importance of a book on tithing such as the one you are reading now.

We will deal now with some of the questions on tithing that I found on the blogosphere.

- *Why is there no mention of tithing in Abraham's life before Genesis 14?*
- *Why do Church leaders use Malachi chapter three to scare believers into tithing, when it is obvious that Malachi was talking to believers who lived under the Law?*

- *Why do Church leaders tell us that we are cursed if we do not tithe when the book of Galatians tells us that Christ became a Curse for us when He hung on the cross?*
- *Why do prosperity teachers tell us to give a tithe of our money when Abraham only gave Melchizedek a tithe of other people's stuff?*
- *Abraham's tithe to Melchizedek was a once-only event, so why do pastors make their church members tithe from their weekly income?*
- *Why do prosperity preachers (or pastors) insist that we give God his 10%, when under the New Testament God owns the entire 100%?*
- *Why do some prosperity teachers use Jacob's reference to tithing in Genesis 28:11-17 to endorse tithing under the New Testament, when it is clear that Jacob was bargaining with God, and bargaining with God is a sin?*

Before I dive into answering these very sobering questions on tithing; let us take a quick look at two of the misleading teachings on tithing that found on the blogosphere under the titles, "Which one was justified?" and "Tithes are 'Corban."

Which one was Justified?

Jesus taught us about two men, one of whom tithed and one of whom did not. "Two men went up into the Temple to pray, one a Pharisee, and the other a tax-gatherer. The Pharisee stood, and was praying thus to himself, 'God I thank Thee that I am not like other people: swindlers, unjust, adulterers, or even like this tax-gatherer. I fast twice a week; I pay tithes of all I get.' But the tax-gatherer, standing some distance away, was beating his breast, saying, 'God, be merciful to me, the sinner!' I tell you, this man went down to his house justified rather than the other; for everyone who exalts himself shall be humbled, but he who humbles himself shall be exalted (Luke 18:10-14)."

❧❧❧❧❧❧❧

***Tithing is not a license to walk in pride before
the LORD, because He resists the proud.***

❧❧❧❧❧❧❧

So which one was justified before God, the tither or the non-tither? This was the questioned posed by the author who chose to remain anonymous. In the above quote, the author of the article is attempting to use the passage of Scripture from the eighteenth chapter of the book of Luke to lead his readers in the blogosphere into believing that Jesus was using the story in this passage to demonstrate that under the New Testament God justifies non-tithers rather than tithers. Nothing could be further from the truth, but I have to give the author an "A" plus for having a very over-reaching imagination. To the contrary, Luke 18:10-14 is a lesson on the importance of humility and the dangers of self-righteousness.

God justified the tax-gatherer in the story, not because he did not pay tithes, but because he sincerely humbled himself before God. This passage of Scripture is a lesson on the power of humility before God and was never intended to marginalize or undermine tithing. However, this passage also contains a veiled warning to all "tithers," which is this: tithing is not a license to walk in pride before the LORD, because He resists the proud and gives grace to the humble. I am convinced that some Christians are not experiencing the benefits of tithing because they tithe from pride, instead of tithing with humility before God.

Tithes are 'Corban'

"He was also saying to them, "You nicely set aside the commandment of God in order to keep your tradition. For Moses said, 'Honor your father and your mother'; and, 'He who speaks evil of father or mother, let him be put to death'; but you say, 'If a man says to his father, anything of mine you might have been helped by is Corban (that is to say, given to God), 'you no longer permit him to do anything for his father or his mother; thus invalidating the word of God by your tradition which you have handed down; and you do many such things as that." Mark 7:9-13

"If you have money your family needs, but you withhold it from them in order to pay it to the church as 'tithes,' you are doing exactly what the Pharisees did. You are saying that your money is 'Corban' and Jesus taught that by doing so you were invalidating the Word of God." (Author unknown)

In the above quote, our unknown author from the blogosphere is now attempting to show his readers that giving tithes to the Church while our family needs money is doing the exact same thing that the Pharisees did when they placed the traditions of men above the infallible Word of God. Again nothing could be further from the truth. To the contrary, the above passage is a strong rebuke to religious leaders who compromised on applying the full counsel of the Word of God because they were taking bribes from the people. Jesus was letting the Pharisees know that tithes and offerings that were collected from the people in exchange for turning a blind eye to other important matters of the Law, were not only tainted but such actions were nullifying the power of God's Word in people's lives. It is clear from our unknown author's interpretation of the passage of Scripture from Mark 7:9-13, that the author suffers from a spiritual disease called "humanism."

"Since the fall of Adam and Eve, man's greatest besetting sin is the sin of "humanism." Humanism is a demonic ideology that places the "needs of a human being" above what God's requires from every human. Humanism is a work of the flesh, and it is rooted in "self-centeredness." When the Scriptures fall into the hands of theologians who interpret the Scriptures through the "eyes of humanism," preserving man's interest using the Scriptures takes on immediate precedence and the Scriptures suddenly lose their heavenly perspective. If we were to take our unknown author's reasoning we would have to come to the conclusion that the prophet Elijah manipulated the widow of Zarephath in 1 Kings 17:8-15, when he challenged her to give him the first portion of her last piece of bread, when she had a son to take care of. According to the reasoning of our unknown author, the widow's offering was "Corban" and invalidated the Word of God because she gave the first portion of her last piece of bread to a man of God when her family clearly needed it.

~~~~~~~
*"Since the fall of Adam and Eve, man's greatest
besetting sin is the sin of "humanism."*
~~~~~~~

Based upon our unknown author's spiritual ideology, the portion the
widow woman gave to the prophet Elijah would have been well served by
saving it for her starving son. If the prophet Elijah had the same mindset
that our unknown author possesses, the miracle of supernatural supply
in the midst of a famine that is gloriously recorded in the Scriptures
would never have been recorded. What are unknown author and many
of his or her followers in the blogosphere, who are against tithing fail to
realize, is that man's needs are always met in all sufficiency when he or
she is willing to obey God's voice and abide by His eternal principles
as outlined in His Word. Obeying an instruction from God – however
ridiculous it may seem – is the quickest and surest way to meet even the
most desperate of human needs.

What is more, God always chooses and delegates His authority to
a man or woman of His choice. These chosen vessels (Ephesians 4:11)
become God's delegated authorities in the earth, and when we heed
the Word of the Lord through the mouth of these "sent ones," untold
blessings can occur in our lives. Contrary to what the false prophets in
the blogosphere would have us believe, submitting ourselves to God's
delegated authority is not another form of "spiritual bondage." Had the
widow of Zarephath not heeded the Prophet Elijah's admonition, she
would have missed a great blessing from the Lord. Even though she
did not see the Lord physically, God had come to her in physical form
through one of His holy prophets.

Give 10% or 100% — Which is which?

*"The earth is the Lord's, and everything in it. The world and all its
people belong to him."* Psalm 24:1

One of the favorite arguments fronted by those who would have us
believe that tithing was done away with under the New Testament, goes

like this: "We do not have to give our tithes to the Church under the New Testament because everything we own belongs to the Lord anyway. God does not want our ten percent; He just wants all of us. We do not need to tithe under the New Testament because we can all be led by the Holy Spirit to give freewill offerings as the need arises." Taken at face value, these statements by the anti-tithing crowd seem quite reasonable and spiritual. However, further investigation will quickly reveal that these "spiritual sound bites" are the same "spiritual mantras" propagated by the spiritual prophets of "humanism."

In my many years of apostolic service to the Lord, I have yet to come across anyone who opposes tithing under the New Testament who opposed the notion of giving ten percent of their income to the Church, because it hindered them from giving "more than the stipulated ten percent." I have been a pastor for a while, and I have yet to come across anyone who opposes tithing who has ever told me, "Dr. Myles I am tired of being restricted to giving only ten percent of my income, when I really desire to give away 50 or 100% of my income to the kingdom of God." To the contrary, when I checked the giving records of those who are opposed to the giving of tithes, I discovered that they are usually the stingiest givers in the entire congregation. Most of them hardly give away 2% of their income to the work of the Lord, if at all.

I have come to the sobering conclusion that those who oppose tithing under the New Testament and are quick to relegate it to the Old Testament, do not do so solely out of a sincere desire to correct what they perceive as an incorrect doctrine taught by the Church. Any theological objections they have to the biblical practice of tithing are just a well-designed mask to hide their real motives. Their real motives are rooted in plain old greed and self-preservation. These people have a serious love affair with their "money" and the amount of freewill offerings that they give to the work of the Lord, compared to those who believe in tithing, clearly underscores my foregone conclusion. If they truly believed that under the New Testament God wants their 100%, they would be some of the greatest givers to the work of the Lord, but sadly they are not.

෧෨෧෨෧෨෧

I discovered that non-tithers are usually the
stingiest givers in the entire congregation.

෧෨෧෨෧෨෧

Tracing the Prophetic Element in the Scriptures

"Surely the Lord God will do nothing without revealing His secret to His servants the prophets." Amos 3:7

One of the biggest problems that many self-appointed theologians in the blogosphere and in the Church world have, that hinders their ability to properly interpret the Scriptures does not understand the "deep and far-reaching prophetic element" that weaves itself throughout the Scriptures. This prophetic element in the Scriptures requires a "prophetic hearing ear and seeing eye" to really capture many of the hidden meanings of Scripture.

"The hearing ear, and the seeing eye, the LORD hath made even both of them." Proverbs 20:12 (KJV)

King Solomon points out that the LORD has made provision for His children to have both a "hearing ear and a seeing eye." Why would God do such a thing? It is because God knows that much of the spiritual treasures that He has hidden in His Word for our benefit would be lost if we are not able to see "beyond the obvious meaning of a certain scriptural verse or passage." For instance, the passage of Scripture below from the book of Corinthians has a deeper meaning beyond the obvious.

"...and all of them drank the same spiritual water. For they drank from the spiritual rock that traveled with them, and that rock was Christ." 1 Corinthians 10:4

In this wonderful passage of Scripture, the apostle Paul is referring to the people of Israel who came out of Egypt with the prophet Moses. While the children of Israel were journeying to the Promised Land, they passed through the Arabian Desert and at some point during their journey they experienced a serious shortage of water. When the children of Israel became thirsty, they cried to the Lord and to Moses for water. God instructed the prophet Moses to strike a certain "rock," and when he did, water came out of the rock. The children of Israel drank from the rock until they were satisfied.

> *"I will stand before you on the rock at Mount Sinai. Strike the rock, and water will come gushing out. Then the people will able to drink. So Moses struck the rock as he was told, and water gushed out as the elders looked on."* Exodus 17:6

Looking at the above passage of Scripture at face value, it would seem that its interpretation is an "open and shut case." Moses struck the rock, and God supernaturally caused the rock to release water. What else is there? However, when the apostle Paul looks at this same passage of Scripture, he comes up with an "interpretation" that only someone with a "hearing ear and seeing eye" can come up with. Paul tells us that the rock that Moses struck that released the water that refreshed and sustained the children of Israel in the wilderness was "Christ." In this case, the "rock" is the "prophetic element," while "Christ" is the "substantiation" of this prophetic element. Without understanding the "deep and far-reaching prophetic elements" in the Scriptures, "important biblical truths" that are interconnected from the Old Testament to the New become "lost in translation."

When I read most of the articles that were posted by those who are against tithing in the blogosphere, I quickly discovered that their erroneous assumptions were rooted in their inability to account for the "prophetic element" in the writings of Scripture. Many of them failed to perceive the "prophetic symbolism" of Abram's tithe to Melchizedek in Genesis 14. Many of them also failed to see the connection between the Old Testament priestly Order of Melchizedek and the eternal priestly ministry of our Lord Jesus Christ. They also failed to "see" the "deep and far-reaching prophetic elements in the practice of tithing." This is why they can easily relegate tithing to the Old Testament and bury this "incredible spiritual technology for a breakthrough" into the coffin of something that died with the Law of Moses. If you are truly seeking for a "more excellent way" of tithing, I believe that this book will put to rest all your previous questions on the subject of tithing.

๙๖๙๖๙๖๙

Many people fail to perceive the "prophetic symbolism" of Abram's tithe to Melchizedek in Genesis 14.

๙๖๙๖๙๖๙

The Order of Melchizedek

"So too Christ (the Messiah) did not exalt Himself to be made a high priest, but was appointed and exalted by Him Who said to Him, You are My Son; today I have begotten You; ⁶As He says also in another place, You are a Priest [appointed] forever after the order (with the rank) of Melchizedek." Hebrews 5:5-6 (AMP)

Without understanding the deep-and-far-reaching prophetic element that weaves itself through the pages of Scripture, we will fail to recognize just how powerful Abram's meeting with Melchizedek in Genesis 14 really was. Abram's meeting with Melchizedek in the valley of Shaveh (Valley of kings) was one of the most important "God encounters" that any man could ever have. In a later chapter, we will examine "all the prophetic elements" that are hidden in this life-changing meeting in Abram's life and how it affects us today. We will discover why Abram was inspired to tithe into the life and ministry of this lofty High Priest of God Most High. What is abundantly clear is that under the New Testament, believers are not under the Order of Levi, we are under the Order of Melchizedek. This means that tithing must also follow the same pattern.

LIFE APPLICATION SECTION

Point to Ponder:

Humanism is a demonic ideology that places the "needs of a human being or people" above God's interests.

Memory Verse:

"So too Christ (the Messiah) did not exalt Himself to be made a high priest, but was appointed and exalted by Him Who said to Him, You are My Son; today I have begotten You; [6]As He says also in another place, You are a Priest [appointed] forever after the order (with the rank) of Melchizedek." Hebrews 5:5-6

Reflections:

1. Why are some people so determined to relegate tithing to the Old Testament?

_____

_____

_____

_____

2. Is there a mention of tithing in the New Testament?

_____

_____

_____

_____

3. Can you write down the passages of Scripture where tithing is mentioned in the New Testament?

_____

_____

_____

_____

Chapter Four

Debunking the Malachi Tithing System

"Will a man rob God? Yet you have robbed Me! But you say, 'In what way have we robbed You?' In tithes and offerings. ⁹ You are cursed with a curse, For you have robbed Me, Even this whole nation. Malachi 3:8-9

While I disagree with many in the blogosphere and in the Church world who believe that there is no need for tithing under the New Testament, I also have to admit that I completely agree with many in the blogosphere who believe that Malachi 3 is an erroneous foundation for teaching tithing to New Testament believers. I truly believe that the Church's usage of Malachi 3:8-12 as the primary foundation for tithing in the global Church is quite misleading and self-defeating. It is quite sad that some of our greatest prosperity teachers have built their whole ministry around this highly misunderstood passage from the book of Malachi.

There is a "more excellent pattern of tithing" that is applicable to post-Calvary New Testament believers, that clearly transcends the dictates of Malachi 3 and the covenant of Levi. If the global church does not "divorce its tithing model" from the tithing passage in Malachi 3, the "downward trend in tithing" in the global church will only get worse. To help the Church divest and divorce itself from this inaccurate tithing model, I will "systematically" take you through a quick overview of the book of Malachi. In order to do this effectively, we must understand one of the most important principles of writing.

In order for any author to be effective in what he or she is trying to communicate, the author must first know his or her primary audience. Who the "audience" is determines to a large extent the contextual framework of the author's work. An author's audience determines both the subject and content. When we attempt to separate a book that was written to a very specific audience from its intended audience, we are in essence "hijacking" the original author's primary intent. So here are two important questions that demand "surgical answers."

••••••

There is a "more excellent pattern of tithing" that is applicable to post-Calvary New Testament believers

••••••

Two Fundamental Questions

- Who was the prophet Malachi's primary target audience?

- What was his main objective for writing the book of Malachi?

To answer the first question let us examine the following passages of Scripture from the book of Malachi closely.

"A son honors his father, and a servant his master. If then I am a Father, where is My honor? And if I am a Master, where is the [reverent] fear due Me? says the Lord of hosts to you, O priests, who despise My name. You say, How and in what way have we despised Your name? 8When you [priests] offer blind [animals] for sacrifice, is it not evil? And when you offer the lame and the sick, is it not evil? Present such a thing [a blind or lame or sick animal] now to your governor [in payment of your taxes, and see what will happen]. Will he be pleased with you? Or will he receive you graciously? says the Lord of hosts. 9Now then, I [Malachi] beg [you priests], entreat God [earnestly] that He will be gracious to us. With such a gift from

your hand [as a defective animal for sacrifice], will He accept it or show favor to any of you? says the Lord of hosts." Malachi 1:6-9 (AMP)

A quick and honest examination of the first chapter in Malachi quickly unmasks the prophet Malachi's primary target audience. The book of Malachi, contrary to what is taught by many prosperity teachers, was not written to rebuke the children of Israel (the 11 none priestly tribes) who were robbing God of His tithes and offerings. To the contrary, the prophet Malachi was rebuking many of the members of the Levitical priestly order who were mishandling the Lord's tithes and offerings. These wayward "priests" were stealing from God by sacrificing animals with blemishes to God while keeping the best animals for personal consumption. This dishonorable behavior by the Levites had seriously grieved the heart of God and placed the entire priesthood of Levi in serious jeopardy. God even asked these wayward priests why they did not honor Him like a son is supposed to honor his father.

"AND NOW, O you priests, this commandment is for you. ² If you will not hear and if you will not lay it to heart to give glory to My name, says the Lord of hosts, then I will send the curse upon you, and I will curse your blessings; yes, I have already turned them to curses because you do not lay it to heart." Malachi 2:1-2

"For the priest's lips should guard and keep pure the knowledge [of My law], and the people should seek (inquire for and require) instruction at his mouth; for he is the messenger of the Lord of hosts." Malachi 2:7

By the time we roll over to the second chapter of Malachi, it becomes increasingly clear that the prophet Malachi's "rod of correction" was designed to chastise members of the Levitical priesthood who were misrepresenting God. What is even more interesting is that the famous mantra of many prosperity teachers, "you will be cursed with a curse if you do not tithe" was actually referring to the "curse" that God had pronounced in Malachi 2:2. God had already promised that He would allow a curse to come upon the Levites if they did not repent from their evil deeds. If this one consideration does not debunk the Church's usage of Malachi 3 as its primary basis for its tithing model, then we have become "dull of hearing." God promised to "curse the blessings of the Levites." The million-dollar question is, "What was the blessing of the Levites?"

Simply put, the blessing of the Levites was their unfettered "access to the presence of God" and every ancillary benefit that came from serving in God's temple. God was, in essence, telling the Levites that "if they don't repent" He would remove the "access" that they had to His presence. Special access to God's presence was the only reason the children of Israel gave "tithes" to the Levites. If they lost access to God's presence, who would honestly give them tithes? They would essentially lose their perceived spiritual value in the eyes of the children of Israel.

✿✿✿✿✿✿

The blessing of the Levites was their unfettered "access to the presence of God"

✿✿✿✿✿✿

"But you have turned aside out of the way; you have caused many to stumble by your instruction [in the law]; you have corrupted the covenant of Levi [with Me], says the Lord of hosts. [7]Even from the days of your fathers you have turned aside from My ordinances and have not kept them. Return to me, and I will return to you, says the Lord of hosts. But you say, How shall we return? [8]Will a man rob or defraud God? Yet you rob and defraud Me. But you say, In what way do we rob or defraud You? [You have withheld your] tithes and offerings. [9]You are cursed with the curse, for you are robbing Me, even this whole nation. [10]Bring all the tithes (the whole tenth of your income) into the storehouse, that there may be food in My house, and prove Me now by it, says the Lord of hosts, if I will not open the windows of heaven for you and pour you out a blessing, that there shall not be room enough to receive it." Malachi 3:6-10 (AMP)

By the time we finally get to the third chapter of Malachi, which is the Church's most favorite chapter on tithing, it is now embarrassingly clear that the prophet Malachi has not changed the object of his "harsh rebuke." Contrary to what many prosperity preachers teach, Malachi chapter three is not a "stand-alone" chapter. It is not independent of the prophet Malachi's ongoing rebuke against an ailing priesthood. In Malachi 3:6 God deepens His harsh rebuke of the sinning Levites when He accuses them of stumbling many of the people of Israel and corrupting the covenant God had made with the tribe of Levi. One does not have to be a rocket scientist to figure out the obvious. Malachi chapter three in its most accurate context was not written to correct the "lack of tithing" among the laity in Israel. The passage from Malachi 3:8-12 was God's final verdict on the Levitical priests who did not repent of robbing God of His tithes and offerings.

4 Levels of Tithing Under the Levitical Priesthood

"A priest—a descendant of Aaron—will be with the Levites as they receive these tithes. And a tenth of all that is collected as tithes will be delivered by the Levites to the Temple of our God and placed in the storerooms." Nehemiah 10:38

Many believers in Christendom and some preachers of the gospel do not know that under the priestly Order of Aaron there were several levels or layers of tithing. Let us list these levels or layers of tithing for the sake of our study.

- There was a tithe the general population of Israel gave to the Levites. (Numbers 18:21)
- There was a tithe of the tithe that the Levites gave to the High Priestly Order of Aaron. (Numbers 18:25-31)
- The people of Israel kept a tithe to pay for their annual pilgrimage to Jerusalem. (Deut 14:22-26)
- The people paid a tithe to take care of the poor, the orphans and the widows. (Deut 14:28-29)

Once we understand these four layers of tithing under the priestly Order of Aaron, understanding the proper context of Malachi 3 becomes quite easy. When God posed the questions "Will a man rob God? And ye say wherein have we robbed you?" God quickly answered, "in tithes and offerings." Who was God really talking about? Contrary to the popular teachings on this passage, God was not accusing the laity in Israel of robbing Him of His tithes and offerings. He was accusing the "priests" (pastors or spiritual leaders of Israel) of robbing Him of tithes and offerings.

The passage from the book of Nehemiah 10:38 completely solves the mystery of Malachi 3:8-10. The prophet Nehemiah identifies the "storehouse" that the prophet Malachi was alluding to in the third chapter of Malachi. According to the Law of Moses, the Levites were instructed by Moses under divine decree to give a "tithe of the tithe" to the household of Aaron. Members of the household of Aaron were the only ones among the Levites who were appointed by God to the office of High Priest. They lived on a "tithe" of all the "tithes" that the Levites collected from all the tribes of Israel.

During the prophet Malachi's era some of the members of the Levitical priesthood were so corrupt that they were not giving the household of Aaron their rightful portion of the tithe of the tithes. This behavior so grieved the heart of God that He sent the prophet Malachi with a harsh word of rebuke. When church leaders apply Malachi chapter three to lay people in the Church, they are really "overstretching the text." Those who are very zealous for Malachi 3 need to use it to rebuke pastors who do not tithe. Speaking frankly, some pastors do not tithe and many who do tithe, tithe incorrectly. Any senior pastor who tithes into his own church is tithing incorrectly. The "tithe" does not "go down" it "goes up!" I will discuss this principle fully in a later chapter. Malachi chapter 3 is more suited to rebuking pastors who do not tithe into their spiritual covering than for rebuking lay people in the Church who do not tithe. That said, every child of God is called to "tithe" to the Lord.

ৡৡৡৡৡৡ
When church leaders apply Malachi 3 to lay people in the Church, they are really "overstretching the text."
ৡৡৡৡৡৡ

"[Earnestly] remember the law of Moses, My servant, the statutes and the ordinances which I commanded him on [Mount] Horeb [to give] to all Israel." Malachi 4:4 (AMP)

We have finally reached the point where we can answer our second question. "What was the Prophet Malachi's primary objective for writing the book of Malachi?" The answer to this vital question stares us in the face when we read Malachi 4:4. The Prophet Malachi wanted the ailing Levitical priesthood to "remember the Law of Moses." Stated simply, everything the prophet Malachi wrote in the book of Malachi was designed to help the priests who were falling short of their calling and duty to remember the Law of Moses. Nothing could be clearer than this. So here is my challenge to you: "Are you under the Law of Moses or are you under grace?" If you believe that you are under the Law of Moses then have fun "remembering the Law of Moses." The word "remember" literally means to "put the original parts back together (reassemble)." It is clear to me that we can no longer preach the gospel of the Kingdom and live under the "dispensation of grace," while continuing to tithe according to the Law of Moses.

Money: The lowest asset in the Kingdom of God

The "undue emphasis" on money as one of the primary benefits of tithing is one of the major flaws in the teaching on tithing that is based upon the "Malachi 3:8-12 model." Proponents of the Malachi 3:8-12 pattern of tithing are quick to inform their listeners that the primary benefit of tithing is "the supernatural acquisition of more money" in their personal economy. As a consequence, the primary penalty for not tithing is the manifestation of a "financial curse" over the personal economy of those who refuse to pay the Lord's tithe. This kind of undue emphasis on money as one of the primary benefits of tithing has become the source of "much frustration and debate" among many believers in the blogosphere and in the global Church. The lack of tangible financial resources in the lives of some very faithful tithers clearly indicates that "acquiring more money" is not the primary benefit of tithing as far as God is concerned. I do not mean to discourage "faithful tithers" by my previous statement.

However, let me ask you a very important question. If God gave you the "choice" to choose between "more money" or getting "true heavenly riches" that money cannot buy; what would you choose?

This undue emphasis of making money the primary benefit of tithing by those who use the "Malachi 3:8-12 Tithing system" has "frustrated and disenfranchised" many faithful tithers. Many of these faithful tithers feel like failures because "monetarily" they are still not as rich as they would like to be. Many of them have been tithing for years and yet have experienced dismal improvement in their personal economy. This undue emphasis on money in the Malachi 3:8-12 tithing model, has also helped to produce a second group of believers in the blogosphere who are even more determined not to tithe, because the way the church teaches tithing in its present form does not sufficiently explain why the world is full of rich people like Arab Sheiks, Bill Gates or Steve Jobs who have never "paid" any tithes to God.

ৠ৾৾৾৾৾৾৾

***"Acquiring more money" is not the primary
benefit of tithing as far as God is concerned.***

ৠ৾৾৾৾৾৾৾

Furthermore, common experience has also shown us that there are also some "wealthy Christians" who attend church regularly but do not tithe regularly, if at all. Nevertheless, they seem to continue to "prosper financially." How do we explain this seemingly contradictory phenomenon to the "tithing" faithful? Imagine telling Oprah Winfrey, Bill Gates and Donald Trump that they will be cursed with a financial curse if they do not tithe? They would laugh us to scorn and conclude that we are mentally challenged. Why? They have already made billions of dollars without tithing, as they are for the most part unchurched. I will show you in a later chapter that becoming financially wealthy through tithing is a by-product of "tithing correctly" and "accessing" what Jesus called "true riches" as the Holy Spirit responds to our faithfulness.

"If therefore ye have not been faithful in the unrighteous mammon, who will commit to your trust true riches?" Luke 16:11

Why are there so many wealthy people in the world who have never given God His proper endowment of tithe?

The answer to this seemingly perplexing question is simple but deeply profound in its spiritual ramification. If we let the holy book speak for itself, it becomes abundantly clear that Jesus never regarded "money" as one of the highest assets in the Kingdom of God. To the contrary, Jesus called money, "unrighteous mammon." This expression that the Lord Jesus Christ used to describe money does not mean that money by itself is "evil."

To the contrary, Jesus used this expression to indicate that "money" is the lowest spiritual asset in God's Kingdom economy because it is manufactured in the "realms of unrighteousness." More importantly God never "created money." Mankind as a way of effecting interpersonal trade after Adam and Eve lost "access" to the original kingdom economy that God had established for them in the Garden of Eden, created money. Ever since the fall of Adam and Eve, the world we live in has fallen into the zone of "unrighteousness." Money is found in abundance in this realm of "unrighteousness." This is why thieves can simply break into a house or bank and come out with loads of cash. Money is so common in the "realms of unrighteousness," such that men and women can turn to their basest instincts and still have the capacity to "capture money."

For example, a woman can choose to wear very seductive attire and parade herself before the eyes of lustful men. Money in exchange for sex is the multibillion-dollar industry of our times. I can assure you that within a couple of days of selling her body, this woman will probably make more money than many God-fearing people make for an entire year! A bank robber, on the other hand, can break into a bank and walk away with more money than many faithful tithers will ever make in an entire lifetime. How is this possible? The answer is simple. Money is the lowest asset in God's economy because it is the creation of a fallen man. Jesus told us that "money" is not even included on the list of what Jesus called "true riches." If money is the lowest asset in God's economy, why is it that those who teach tithing according to Malachi 3:8-12, give it a place of uttermost importance? It is quite clear that money is the number one prized asset in the "Babylonian systems of human government." The Holy Spirit told me, "Francis any tithing system that makes getting money the primary benefit of tithing is demonic in nature and can easily be attacked by the demonic powers."

Money is found in abundance in this realm of "unrighteousness."

Thankfully, in God's faithful estimation, money comes right after we have exhausted the list of "true riches." This is why any tithing system that says that the acquisition of money is the primary benefit of tithing is inherently flawed and out of touch with God's divine kingdom order. God created the tithe to give tithers access to heaven's "true riches" and the "supernatural acquisition of money" as one of the benefits of tithing would then be a distant second. Getting "more money" is a by-product of tithing for the right reasons, in the same way that a Nigerian oil refinery ends up with valuable by-products such as soap while the company is trying to refine crude oil. This book will show you why God waited until Abraham was very rich in gold and silver before introducing him to the Kingdom concept of tithing. I do not want to be misconstrued as saying that "tithing can never make a person prosper financially." To the contrary, I believe that tithing does invoke upon the believer a "special grace" to prosper financially. However, getting more money is not the primary benefit of tithing. When the Holy Spirit was "debunking the Malachi 3 tithing system" He told me to take a fresh look at many of the proposed benefits of tithing under the Malachi chapter 3 tithing system.

Windows Are For Those Who Are On The Outside

Bring all the tithes into the storehouse, that there may be food in My house, and try Me now in this," Says the Lord of hosts, "If I will not open for you the windows of heaven and pour out for you such blessing that there will not be room enough to receive it. Malachi 3:10

According to Malachi 3, one of the benefits of "tithing" under the Levitical priesthood was the "opening of the windows of heaven." I used to love this "tithing promise" when I used to rely on Malachi 3 to exact the tithe from members of my church. However, my enthusiasm changed drastically when the LORD gave me a revelation about the Order of Melchizedek priesthood. One day the LORD dropped a bombshell revelation in my spirit. He said to me, "Francis, windows are for people who live on the outside. If you are being fed through windows, it means you are operating from the outside." This stunned me. I had never seen before.

The LORD the reminded me of the apartheid days in South Africa when Black people (or races considered inferior to White people) were paid their "salaries" through windows, while White employees went through the door to collect their paycheck. Suddenly I saw it! The opening of the windows of heaven was not such a great blessing after all. It was simply the "best" God could give the children of Israel under the dispensation of Law before Jesus re-introduced fallen humanity to the gospel of the Kingdom. Furthermore, the LORD said to me, "Francis, why do you need Me to feed you through windows when Christ the "Door" to the Kingdom has arrived?"

❧❧❧❧❧❧

Windows are for people who live on the outside.
If you are being fed through windows, it
means you are operating from the outside."

❧❧❧❧❧❧

In the book of John, Jesus declared, "I am the door. If anyone enters by Me, he will be saved, and will go in and out and find pasture. The thief does not come except to steal, and to kill, and to destroy. I have come that they may have life, and that they may have it more abundantly (John 10:9-10). The Holy Spirit then challenged me to investigate the New Testament and see if the word "window" is ever used in relation to a blessing from God. I was stunned because the word "window" does not appear anywhere in the New Testament as a covenantal blessing. The only places where the word "window" is used in the New Testament is in Acts 20:9, when a young man fell from a window after he fell asleep while listening to Paul the apostle. The second reference is 2

Corinthians 11:33, when Paul the apostle had to escape certain death by being let down through a window. Ironically both stories show us what happens to New Testament believers who live through "windows."

From Open Windows to Open Doors

*"I know your works. See, I have set before you **an open door**, and no one can shut it; for you have a little strength, have kept My word, and have not denied My name.* Revelation 3:8

*After these things I looked, and behold, **a door standing open** in heaven. And the first voice, which I heard was like a trumpet speaking with me, saying, "Come up here, and I will show you things which must take place after this."* Revelation 4:1

Thankfully, in the New Testament, the word "window" as a spiritual technology for engaging the blessings of God is quickly replaced by a more powerful spiritual technology, "accessing the covenantal blessings of God through an open door!" I quickly realized that in the New Testament the covenant blessings of the LORD are connected to the word "Door!" In the New Testament "open windows of heaven" give way to "open doors in the heavenly realms." Which one of these spiritual technologies do you think is more superior?

The Holy Spirit then dropped the final bombshell when He dropped this thought in my spirit. "Francis, the biggest furniture in your house did not come through windows. It came through doors." It was all I could do not to scream. I realized then that "tithing under the Order of Melchizedek" does not open windows of blessings, it opens "doors of blessings." Hallelujah! Unfortunately, Sunday after Sunday, well-meaning pastors encourage their congregants to tithe for " open windows" instead of tithing for "open doors." Its no wonder the tithers are not getting much out of their tithing. We keep limiting how much God can give us by the power of our own confession. "You are snared

35

by the words of your mouth; You are taken by the words of your mouth." (Proverbs 6:2)

Tithes According to the Law

And indeed those who are of the sons of Levi, who receive the priesthood, have a commandment to receive tithes from the people according to the law, that is, from their brethren, though they have come from the loins of Abraham; Hebrews 7:5

The writer of the book of Hebrews makes it clear that Levi was commanded by God to collect "tithes" from his brethren (the children of Israel) according to the Law. This statement demands that we investigate it with forensic aptitude. The spiritual implications of this statement are far-reaching and sobering. No one understood the differences between the dispensation of Law and Grace, like the Apostle Paul. Why? He was a Pharisee and zealous advocate of the Law of Moses. So when Paul writes… "Christ is the end of the law to everyone who believes (Romans 10:4)." This is a clear statement that you cannot mix the Law and Grace, because the engines of faith fuel the latter. The Law is the "shadow of things to come" whereas "Grace" is the essence of everything foreshadowed by the Law. On the other hand faith is the substance of things hoped for and the evidence of things not seen (Hebrews 11:1). "For by grace you have been saved through faith, and that not of yourselves; it is the gift of God, not of works, lest anyone should boast (Ephesians 2:8-9)."

In the New Testament "open windows of heaven"
give way to "open doors in the heavenly realms."

It's quite interesting to see "faith teachers" make the "faithful" come under bondage to the Law of Moses during the collection of tithes. This is due to the fact that no matter how we try to clean it up, Malachi 3 is describing a "tithing system" according to the Law. This means that whether pastors like it or not, each time they draw their tithes by appealing to Malachi; they unknowingly suck "the oxygen of grace and faith" out of the whole practice of tithing.

Consequently, it's not surprising that many of their congregants still struggle to "exercise faith" consistently in the area of tithing. Abraham never tithed to Melchizedek because the Law compelled him. He was only compelled by faith and divine revelation. There was no "Law" when Abram met Melchizedek. Abraham's motivation for tithing into Melchizedek was much loftier than simply obeying the dictates of Law. Many Christians tithe more from "fear" than from a desire to honor the God who has blessed them with everything they have. I pray that this book will help destroy that spirit trajectory.

❦❧❦❧❦❧

***The Law is the "shadow of things to come" whereas
"Grace" is the essence of everything foreshadowed by the Law.***

❦❧❦❧❦❧

You Are Under a Curse!

"Will a man rob God? Yet you have robbed Me! But you say, 'In what way have we robbed You?' In tithes and offerings. ⁹ You are cursed with a curse, For you have robbed Me, Even this whole nation. Malachi 3:8-9

This is precisely why I have serious issues with the popular Malachi 3:8-12 system of tithing, because I know that it originates out of the Mountain of Law. Consequently, its spiritual roots are steeped in legalism. The Malachi 3:8-12 system of tithing describes a Levitical tithe, which was paid according to the law. This means that "no matter how we try to spiritualize and decorate the Malachi tithing model to make it applicable to New Testament believers, its true spiritual roots and origins will always lead us back to the Mountain of Law."

Once we head back to the Mountain of Law, the fruit this mountain produces is "legalism." It will inevitably creep into our internal motivation for the giving of "tithes." Before we know it, we will start basing our relationship with a loving God on the basis of whether we gave our tithes or not. A Nigerian pastor friend of mine based in South Africa recently sent me a video, in which a well-known man of God was telling thousands of his pastors, to tell members of their congregation that if they don't "pay their tithes" they are going straight to Hell, when they die. When I saw this video, my heart was broken because this is a father in the faith I respect highly. "When did paying tithes to a church become more precious than Christ's finished work on Calvary's cross?"

❧❧❧❧❧❧❧

***Many Christians tithe more from "fear"
than from a desire to honor the God.***

❧❧❧❧❧❧❧

Unfortunately, the drastic statement from this precious man of God is quite understandable when a preacher is addicted to the Malachi 3 tithing system. The works of the Law will quickly crush and snuff out the precious embers of the flames of grace and faith inside the human heart. Just look at how well-meaning men and women of God curse God's people from the pulpit whenever they start talking about the giving of tithes and offerings.

Blessed be the God and Father of our Lord Jesus Christ, who has blessed us with every spiritual blessing in the heavenly places in Christ. Ephesians 1:3

My skin crawls whenever I hear highly anointed men and women of God pronounce "curses" on their people from the pulpit. With unfeigned passion, they tell their terrified people that they are "cursed" if they do not pay their tithes. Without a doubt, the basis for their harsh pronouncements is Malachi 3:8-12. It's no wonder there is so little joy in tithing in the global Church. What's worse, we fail to discern the true spiritual condition of New Testament believers and just how perfect and complete the finished work of Christ really is.

The Problem of Capacity

Bring all the tithes into the storehouse, that there may be food in My house, and try Me now in this," Says the Lord of hosts, "If I will not open for you the windows of heaven and pour out for you such blessing that there will not be room enough to receive it.
Malachi 3:10

When I was a Malachi tithing teacher, I used to celebrate the above blessing as a very big deal. I no longer do. When the Lord was giving me the revelation about tithing under the Order of Melchizedek, He showed something about this scripture that I had never seen before. He said to me, "Francis look at this passage again. You think its a blessing, but I am actually lamenting the lack of spiritual capacity by the children of Israel under the Old Covenant to receive ALL that I wanted to bless them with." I had never seen it before. Suddenly I saw it! "See if I will not pour out such a blessing…that you do not have enough room (capacity) to receive it (the blessing)." I was stunned. What I thought was a major blessing for tithing under the Malachi model was actually a "limited blessing" at best.

The Holy Spirit showed me that people under the Old Covenant did not have the spiritual capacity to receive all that Heaven wanted to pour out. Why? Because "Christ" (the hope of glory) was not resident in them as He indwells New Testament born-again believers. This means that under the Old Covenant the only "spiritual container" the people had to receive what Heaven had released, was their unregenerate spirits. However, under the New Testament, "Christ" the hope of glory resides in each believer, so He is the "spiritual container" on behalf of the believer for everything the Father in heaven is releasing on Earth. So under Christ's New Testament Melchizedek priesthood tithing believers are not hindered by the problem of "capacity to receive."

People under the Old Covenant did not have the spiritual capacity to receive all that Heaven wanted to pour out.

Have you ever heard overzealous televangelist make this bodacious claim, "God is going to give you a net-breaking harvest." I used to shout with excitement when I heard this, until the day the Lord challenged me on it. He said to me, "a net-breaking harvest is not a blessing. It's a curse. If a is net breaking during harvest; change the capacity of the net." I have never celebrated a net-breaking harvest ever since. The primary problem with a net-breaking harvest is that by the time you get to your "net" the only "evidence" that the LORD had tried to bless you, is a "broken net." Tithing under the Order of Melchizedek unlocks inside of the believer all that Christ can contain. I hope you now realize that the popular Malachi 3 tithing system is not the best tithing system for New Testament believers.

LIFE APPLICATION SECTION

Point to Ponder:

The Malachi tithing system is the not best tithing systems for New Testament believers, since its driven by the law instead of grace.

Memory Verse:

"For the priest's lips should guard and keep pure the knowledge [of My law], and the people should seek (inquire for and require) instruction at his mouth; for he is the messenger of the Lord of hosts." Malachi 2:7

Reflections:

1. Who was the Prophet Malachi's primary target audience, when he wrote the book of Malachi?

_____

_____

_____

_____

2. Why is it erroneous to say that the giving of tithes is "Corban?"

_____

_____

_____

_____

3. What were the four levels of tithing under the Levitical priestly Order?

_____

_____

_____

_____

Chapter Five

Questions on Tithing that Demand Answers?

My people are destroyed for lack of knowledge. Because you have rejected knowledge, I also will reject you from being priest for Me; Because you have forgotten the law of your God, I also will forget your children. Hosea 4:6

Without a doubt, there are many questions many Christians around the world have on the subject of tithing. If it were not the case, tithing wouldn't be such a controversial subject in most churches, regardless of geography. In this chapter, I will deliberately answer many of these questions that are universal in nature. May the precious Holy Spirit give you an hearing "ear" and an "obedient heart."

~Why is there no mention of tithing in Abraham's life before Genesis 14?

"But when the right time came, God sent his Son, born of a woman, subject to the law. 5 God sent him to buy freedom for us who were

slaves to the law, so that he could adopt us as his very own children."
Galatians 4:4-5

God never does anything out of its due season. God has a perfect timing mechanism that He uses to synchronize and deploy all of His eternal purposes here on earth. Every farmer knows that the worst mistake any farmer can make is to attempt to harvest his or her crops before they are ripe for harvest. Waiting for the right time to harvest a fruit tree does not in anyway negate the importance of the fruit itself. In the same manner, God waited until He knew that the right time to introduce the "concept of tithing" to Abram had arrived.

When Abram met Melchizedek (the king-priest) in the valley of Shaveh, he had spiritually matured to the point where he could appreciate the power of the eternal truths that God was introducing to him in this glorious encounter with this lofty High Priest of God Most High. Furthermore, the prevailing circumstances on the ground had divinely lined up to further impress upon Abram's mind the awesome power of the tithe. The fact that God never told Abraham about the tithe in previous chapters does not in anyway negate the sacred importance of the divine enactment of the tithe. Most importantly, God waited until Abram was very rich in gold and silver before introducing him to the Kingdom concept of "tithing." Why? The Holy Spirit told me that God wanted to make sure that Abraham and his descendants do not "connect" tithing to "getting more money." Tithing under the Order of Melchizedek was designed to give Abraham access to "things money cannot buy." Melchizedek's interceptive appearance as the king of Sodom was headed towards Abram created the perfect spiritual environment for introducing humanity to such a powerful Kingdom principle as the "tithe."

☙❧☙❧☙❧

***God waited until He knew that the right time to
introduce the "concept of tithing" to Abram had arrived.***

☙❧☙❧☙❧

~Why do modern Church leaders use Malachi Chapter three to scare or motivate believers into tithing, when it is obvious that Malachi was talking to Levitical priests who lived under the Law of Moses?

I have already answered the above question in the previous pages of this chapter, but I will shed more light on this important question. The main reason why many Church leaders rely heavily on Malachi chapter three as their main basis for teaching or exacting the tithe is staggeringly simple. Many well-meaning spiritual leaders have not had access to a Bible-based teaching book like the one you are reading, which can teach them how to exact the tithe under the Order of Melchizedek, instead of using the Levitical model. Many well-meaning pastors do not know that there is a more excellent way of exacting the tithe under the New Testament.

> *"Tell me, you who want to live under the law, do you know what the law actually says?"* Galatians 4:21

Since the giving of tithes is one of the main sources of funding for the work of the ministry in most churches, pastors have to find a way to teach on the importance of tithing to their flock. Since Malachi 3 seems to present the easiest teaching on tithing, many pastors have found it an easy solution to their dilemma. In the course of writing this book, several great pastors told me: "Dr. Myles, before I heard your teaching or read your book, I had no other alternative for teaching on tithing, even though I did not like telling my flock that they were cursed if they did not tithe."

~Why do Church leaders tell us that we are cursed if we do not tithe, when the book of Galatians tells us that Christ became a Curse for us when He hung on the cross?

"But Christ has rescued us from the curse pronounced by the law. When he was hung on the cross, he took upon himself the curse for our wrongdoing. For it is written in the Scriptures, 'Cursed is everyone who is hung on a tree.'" Galatians 3:13

The above passage of Scripture makes it adamantly clear that New Testament believers have been redeemed from the curse of the Law. To deny this indelible theological fact is tantamount to nullifying the finished work of Christ. Since Malachi 3:8-12 is a passage that refers to the spiritual consequences of not giving the tithe according to the Law, it follows that New Testament believers were also redeemed from this Malachi curse when Christ was hung on the cross and became a curse for us that we might inherit the blessing of Abraham.

On the other hand, I do not want to be misconstrued as suggesting that there are no spiritual consequences for not tithing under the priestly Order of Melchizedek. There are spiritual consequences for not tithing under this eternal priestly Order, which we will explore in great detail in a later chapter. However, these spiritual consequences are deployed on a very different spiritual technology than that of imposing of a curse. The apostle Paul is quite clear in the passage below that under the New Testament priesthood God does not curse His children for any reason. To the contrary, He "chastises or scourges us" when we choose to disobey His Word. This divine chastisement and scourging is effective enough to change the heart and behavior of His dear children. Those of God's children who are beyond the reach of this divine chastisement and scourging are already "reprobate" and have already cursed themselves by resisting the Spirit of God.

"For whom the Lord loveth he chasteneth, and scourgeth every son whom he receiveth. [7] If ye endure chastening, God dealeth with you as with sons; for what son is he whom the father chasteneth not? [8] But if ye be without chastisement, whereof all are partakers, then are ye bastards, and not sons." Hebrews 12:6-8 (KJV)

~Why do prosperity teachers tell us to give a tithe of our money when Abraham only gave Melchizedek a tithe of other people's stuff ?

I will quickly answer the above question by first saying that the one who asked this question is being rather disingenuous. How can anyone give what does not truly belong to them? It does not make sense any way you twist this. How can you say that you gave a gift when you walked into your neighbors' yard and stole one of their bicycles and then give it to the child of another neighbor across the street? You definitely stole the bicycle, but you certainly did not give it. You can never give what you do not own. Giving always carries the connotation of ownership. It is foolish to assume that Abram gave tithes to Melchizedek from "stuff" that did not belong to him. If this were truly the case, then Abram gave Melchizedek, who was both a King and a Priest, a "mockery offering of tithes."

God would have judged Abram harshly for mocking a priest of God Most High; to the contrary, Melchizedek blessed Abram before God.

Secondly, the question above smells of complete ignorance concerning the ancient principles of warfare. In the ancient world that Abram lived in, it was a widely accepted tradition that "a person or a nation had the complete rights of ownership" over whatever they conquered in battle. This principle is littered throughout the pages of Scripture. Even the Lord Jesus Himself alluded to the spiritual validity of this powerful principle of warfare. Listen to this…

"But if I cast out devils by the Spirit of God, then the kingdom of God is come unto you. [29]Or else how can one enter into a strong man's house, and spoil his goods, except he first bind the strong man? and then he will spoil his house." Matthew 12:28-29

❧❧❧❧❧❧

God's children who are beyond the reach of this divine chastisement and scourging are already "reprobate."

❧❧❧❧❧❧

~Abraham's tithe to Melchizedek was a once-only event, so why do pastors make their church members tithe from their weekly income?

At face value, the above question seems like it stands on solid footing. However, further investigation will prove otherwise. Many once-only events in the Bible establish important Kingdom principles and fundamental truths that God intends to play out throughout the whole course of human history.

For instance, God only spoke once in the first chapter of Genesis, when He declared, "Let there be light!" Does this once-only event give us the right to expect the light of the Sun every day since then? Obviously, the answer is yes. The Bible tells us that Jesus Christ died on the cross once-and-for-all. Does this then mean that we cannot preach about the cross of Christ and its ongoing benefits to ensuing generations? Whenever we are dealing with the establishment of precedent, principles and fundamental doctrines, it is not the number of times the subject is mentioned in the Scriptures that matters, as much as the precedent set by the said principle.

> *"Unlike those other high priests, he does not need to offer sacrifices every day. They did this for their own sins first and then for the sins of the people. But Jesus did this once for all when he offered himself as the sacrifice for the people's sins."* Hebrews 7:27

The reason why many pastors challenge the faithful in their flock to give tithes out of their weekly income, is due to the precedent that was set by Abram's initial tithe, which underscores the fact that God's eternal priesthood has a legitimate right to the tithes of whatever Kingdom citizens take possession of in the marketplace. Abram's giving of tithes was his personal acknowledgment that he owed his victory in the battle to God Most High! Most importantly the writer of Hebrews says, "Here (on Earth) mortal men (Levites) receive tithes, but there (in Heaven) he (Jesus) receives them, of whom it is witnessed that he lives (Hebrews 7:8 Emphasis mine)." This passage clearly demonstrates that Jesus as our eternal High Priest is "continuously" receiving "tithes of honor" from His dear children.

Tithing under the Order of Melchizedek is an acknowledgment of Christ's Lordship in the believer's life. It is not a "legal requirement." It is the humble response of an "inspired heart" to the Lordship of Christ. What Abraham did in giving tithes of honor, was no different to what pagan kings did whenever they triumphed in battle. These pagan kings were quick to credit their massive victories to their demon-gods, by giving them substantial sacrificial offerings of blood and other expensive gifts. Melchizedek represented Abraham's God who had given him an incredible victory in the marketplace.

~Why do some prosperity teachers use Jacob's reference to tithing in Genesis 28:11-17 to endorse tithing under the New Testament, when it is quite clear that Jacob was bargaining with God, and bargaining with God is a sin?

Taken at face value, the question above seems to stand on solid footing. However, the truth of the matter is that the answer to our blogger's question is both a "Yes and No" answer. "Yes," bargaining with God over immutable truths and principles that He has clearly revealed to us in His holy word is a sin. This is because such an attitude is a camouflage for the spirit of disobedience. "No," bargaining with God is not a sin, in situations where we are not really sure of His will; especially when our gesture of bargaining with God is made in the spirit of wanting to know God's perfect will for our lives, or when we are interceding for others. We must also not forget that the patriarchs (Abraham, Isaac, and Jacob) did not have the Holy Spirit residing inside them like He resides in the born-again spirits of New Testament believers. The Holy Spirit simply came upon them in brief intervals and then lifted His anointing after communicating His message to them. This is why the patriarchs normally asked God to give them a visible sign that would testify to the truthfulness of the divine encounter that He (God) had given them.

❧❧❧❧❧❧❧

Tithing under the Order of Melchizedek is an acknowledgment of Christ's Lordship in the believer's life.

❧❧❧❧❧❧❧

How many of us have dreamed dreams and have desired to know whether they were from God or not? Let us also not forget that Jacob lived during a time in human history where the people of the ancient world worshipped many demon-gods. These demon-gods would appear to the people of the ancient world in their dreams while they slept. If you were Jacob living under this type of spiritual atmosphere, wouldn't you want proof that the deity that appeared to you in your dream was actually the true and living God whom your forefathers served?

The bargain Jacob made with the God who appeared to him at Bethel was quite prudent of him. Jacob knew from listening to his father Isaac that the God of Abraham was capable of doing what he had asked. Had the God who appeared to Jacob at Bethel failed to satisfy the conditions of Jacob's bargain, Jacob would have simply concluded that He was a "false god" masquerading as the God of Abraham and Isaac. This is why Jacob tied his tithing to the satisfaction of this bargain. Jacob wanted to make sure that he was not tithing to the "wrong God." This would explain why God was not angry with Jacob for suggesting such a bargain. To the contrary, God completely satisfied all the conditions of Jacob's bargain. The passage of Scripture below underscores this very important fact.

> *"I am the God who appeared to you at Bethel, the place where you anointed the pillar of stone and made your vow (promised to tithe) to me. Now get ready and leave this country and return to the land of your birth."* Genesis 31:13 (Emphasis mine)

What is quite revealing is the fact that when God appeared to Jacob many years after appearing to him in a dream at Bethel, God reintroduces Himself as the God who met him at Bethel. God also reminded Jacob of the "vow" that he had made at Bethel. The vow that God was referring to was the "pledge Jacob made to God concerning the giving of tithes." Jacob had promised God that he would give him a tithe (tenth) of all that he had if God satisfied all the conditions of Jacob's bargain. God's reference to this particular "vow" that Jacob made at Bethel underscores two very important facts.

Firstly, it shows that God accepted the conditions of Jacob's bargain. Secondly, it confirms that Jacob's vow to tithe from future provisions of God was the basis for the supernatural blessing that God gave him when he was working for his uncle, Laban. This second fact by itself should forever silence those who say that there is no "spiritual connection" between tithing and the spirit of supernatural provision. This is why using the vow Jacob made to God in Genesis 28:20 to suggest that Jacob 's reference to tithing in this passage doesn't count, because it is the record of a man trying to manipulate God, is overreaching in the interpretation of this powerful passage of Scripture.

Such an assumption is not only absurd, but it also earmarks just how ignorant many believers are of the prevailing spiritual culture of the ancient world. It shows that we are very ignorant of how the people of the ancient world interacted with the deities over their nations. Bargaining (asking for a verifiable sign) with the gods was the quickest to know the power of the said deity. This is exactly what the Prophet Elijah was doing when he challenged the people of his day by saying, "The God who answers by fire, he is the true God" (1 Kings 18).

In conclusion, I want to answer the elephant in the room question, which is the basis for this entire book. The question is, "Is tithing for today?" The answer is a resounding "YES!" However, I admonish you to prayerfully read this entire book before formulating your final opinion, one way or the other. If you desire to discover a "more excellent way of tithing," please read on. If you are the senior pastor or bishop of a church, I pray that God will use this book to help you establish a more excellent way of tithing in your business, congregation or network of churches – a tithing model that is completely "free of legalism," that is "driven by the prophetic streams of divine inspiration in the human heart."

∛∛∛∛

"Is tithing for today?"
The answer is a resounding "YES!"

∛∛∛∛

LIFE APPLICATION SECTION

Point to Ponder:

Tithing was conceived in the heart of God but birthed in the Marketplace. So tithing has marketplace implications.

Memory Verse:

"But when the right time came, God sent his Son, born of a woman, subject to the law. 5 God sent him to buy freedom for us who were slaves to the law, so that he could adopt us as his very own children." Galatians 4:4-5

Reflections:

1. Where did Melchizedek meet Abram?

_____

_____

_____

_____

2. What did Melchizedek bring to the table when He intercepted Abraham?

_____

_____

_____

_____

3. Did God honor the covenant of tithing that Jacob made with God at Bethel?

_____

_____

_____

_____

Chapter Six

The Book of Why?

But Peter said, "Ananias, why has Satan filled your heart to lie to the Holy Spirit and keep back part of the price of the land for yourself? Acts 5:3

When I first wrote this book, this chapter was not part of the original template of my manuscript. One morning, the Holy Spirit woke me up with these words, deeply embedded in my spirit: "The book of Why." I asked the Holy Spirit to explain what He was trying to tell me and the Lord said to me, "In your book on tithing, you must include a chapter called "the book of why." The Holy Spirit told me that in this chapter, he would show me why many born-again believers struggle to tithe consistently. The Lord showed me that the reason why many books lack a heartfelt and meaningful impact on the giving of God's Kingdom citizens is that they focus heavily on the "how to" more than the "question of why?"

The question of "how to" deals with the mechanisms of transport of a particular product or technology. However, the question of "why" deals with the "roots and origins" of an issue at hand. After my time of prayer, I felt a deep impression in my spirit that I was to co-author this particular chapter with my dear friend Dr. Bruce Cook (founder of K.E.Y.S), who is a bona fide marketplace apostle and savvy businessman. Consequently, this chapter is a hybrid of our combined thoughts and prayer on this important issue that affects the body of Christ worldwide.

The Holy Spirit promised to give us some "whys" that are behind the roots and origins of the struggle that the majority of the body of Christ experiences in the area of tithing.

Before doing so, we will first examine the question of "why God created the tithe in the first place?" As a result of the demonic assault by demonic powers on the *Kingdom principle of tithing* and the global proliferation of the "grace message" many pastors have come under tremendous pressure to rename the "tithe" as either "grace giving or first fruits." However, you cannot tamper with God's foreknowledge and not destroy yourself, while forfeiting the spiritual technology behind what God originally intended to establish. God could have easily called "tithes" grace-giving if He had so chosen. As rule of thumb, when it comes to anything God does, the following scripture is what informs my response to it. The passage makes it clear that we are to "seek to understand" what God "does" not try to "change it" to fit the times we live in. God's foreknowledge ensures that whatever He does is ever relevant and has multigenerational implication.

◊◊◊◊◊◊

You cannot tamper with God's Foreknowledge
and not destroy yourself.

◊◊◊◊◊◊

I know that whatever God does, it shall be forever. Nothing can be added to it, And nothing taken from it. God does it, that men should fear before Him. Ecclesiastes 3:14 (Emphasis mine)

Why Did God Create the Tithe?

Let's pause for a moment at the 30,000-foot level before resuming our microscopic analysis and reflect on why God created and established the tithe in order to gain some additional perspective. First, Tithing reflects the unselfish, generous, giving nature of our Creator and Provider. And since we are created in God's image (Gen. 1:26-28), then it is unnatural for us not to give. 2 Cor. 9:6 says: "Whoever sows sparingly will also reap sparingly, and whoever sows generously will also reap generously." Similarly, Proverbs 22:9 says, "A generous man will himself be blessed, for he shares his food with the poor."

The psychologist Abraham Maslow published his famous Hierarchy of Needs, and at the top of the list as the highest level is Self-Actualization. Imagine that! God has hard-wired us, humans, to search and find meaning, purpose, and significance in our existence and one of the primary forms of Self-Actualization for many people is Giving and Philanthropy. Wealthy people often seek to create a legacy or endowment to perpetuate their name or reputation or values to future generations.

From a Kingdom perspective, "Convergence" is a much better term than Self-Actualization. Convergence implies the intersection of gifts, callings, assignments, passions, destiny, maturity, and character, not just how much education or material possessions someone has, or how wealthy they are. The world encourages and reinforces daily in countless ways to each of us the need and desire for humans to be "self-sufficient." This inherent nature and drive of the flesh to focus on self as the center of the universe and to be the master of our own destiny is diametrically opposed to the knowledge and wisdom of God and the example and lifestyle of Jesus.

Finances, intelligence, positional power, physical beauty, and strength are just a few ways that humans express their "self-sufficiency." However, such things do not impress God. God recognized this weakness in us and told Moses to warn the Israelites against this tendency to exalt themselves, thinking: "My power and the strength of my hands [or mind] have produced [gained} this wealth for me." Instead, they were told to "remember the Lord your God, for it is He who gives you the ability [power] to produce [get] wealth, and so confirms his covenant." (Deuteronomy 8:17-18). Furthermore, Jesus told the apostle Paul on one occasion, "My grace is sufficient for you, for my power is made perfect in weakness." (2 Cor. 12:9) After learning this lesson on the sufficiency of Christ, Paul could then write Phil. 3:3-21.

☙✺☙✺☙✺☙

Tithing reflects the unselfish, generous,
giving nature of our Creator and Provider.

☙✺☙✺☙✺☙

Secondly, God does not need our tithe, but we need His protection and provision and resources. God is omniscient, omnipotent, and omnipresent. He owns the cattle on a thousand hills; the gold and silver belong to him. Psalm 50:12 says, "If I were hungry I would not tell you, for the world is mine, and all that is in it." Similarly, in Job 41:11 God asks rhetorically, "Who has a claim against me that I must pay? Everything under heaven belongs to me." So even though the earth has been reserved for man, and we are to exercise dominion, in doing so we are stewards, not owners, of what belongs to God.

Tithing is part of our faith journey and adventure of being a son or daughter in the Kingdom of God and relating to Him in a personal and intimate way, and co-laboring, co-partnering, co-creating, and co-reigning in life in Abba Father's family business. Jesus still calls us out of the boat of comfort and complacency and bids us to walk on the water of life with Him, fixing our eyes on Him and not our circumstances. He calls us to become "impossibility thinkers" rather than "possibility thinkers" (Luke 1:37, 18:27) by the renewing of our minds and hearts in Christ Jesus (Rom. 12:1-2).

Thirdly, Tithing is also a form of joy, honor, and humility. Through willing and cheerful giving (2 Corinthians 9:6-8), we honor and please God. In fact, the Bible says that "God loves a cheerful giver." Some versions translate the word "cheerful" as "hilarious." God wants us to be joyful in our giving; in fact, joy is a weapon and a source of strength for us (Neh. 8:10). "For the kingdom of God is… righteousness, joy, and peace in the Holy Spirit" (Rom. 14:17). We should emphasize that there is great peace that comes from tithing as well. 1 Sam 2:30 says: "Those who honor me I will honor, but those who despise me will be disdained." Proverbs 3:9-10 says, "Honor the Lord with your possessions, and with the firstfruits of your increase, so your barns will be filled with plenty, and your vats will overflow with new wine."

Apostle Robert Henderson has written several excellent books on the power and benefits of firstfruits giving that shed additional light on this form of giving, but our focus here is on tithing. The point is that we honor God with our giving. The Bible teaches us to give honor to whom honor is due (Rom. 13:7)." God as the eternal Creator and Father of all is certainly worthy of honor. Jesus also taught his disciples, "Give to Caesar what is Caesar's, and to God what is God's" (Matt. 22:21). This verse clearly states that certain things belong to God. The tithe is one of them. Since our focus is on tithing, and not offerings, we can only mention in passing that there is also a gift or grace of liberality or generosity available to the body of Christ (Rom. 12:8). Jesus said, "It is more blessed to give than to receive" (Acts 20:35). Those who are experiencing the joy of tithing, as well as other forms of giving, can attest to that.

❧❧❧❧❧❧

God does not need our tithe, but we need His protection and provision and resources.

❧❧❧❧❧❧

Fourthly, God is a God of increase and multiplication. *Tithing is one way that God has designed for His sons and daughters to plant seeds and reap a harvest.* Gen. 8:22 says, "As long as the earth endures, seedtime and harvest, cold and heat, summer and winter, day and night will never cease." 2 Cor. 9:8, 10-11 adds, "And God is able to make all grace abound to you, so that in all things at all times, having all that you need, you will abound in every good work…Now he who supplies seed to the sower and bread for food will also supply and increase your store of seed and will enlarge the harvest of your righteousness. You will be made rich in every way so that you can be generous on every occasion, and through us, your generosity will result in thanksgiving to God."

Every good work, in every way, and on every occasion would certainly include tithing, although the context of this passage of Scripture is a collection for the needy saints in Jerusalem. God clearly wants His children and His Church to be able to sow seed and to reap a Harvest. Tithing is one type of spiritual seed, and seed helps prime the pump in the Kingdom economy, which is based on sowing and reaping rather than buying and selling. Man's creation "Money" is based upon "buying and selling." Jesus said in Luke 6:38: "Give, and it will be given to you. A good measure, pressed down, shaken together and running over, will be poured into your lap. For with the measure you use, it will be measured to you." Although this oft-quoted verse does not specifically mention or address tithing, it displays God's heart toward giving and sets forth cause-and-effect principles.

Fifthly, God is an investor and is looking for sons and daughters who are also investors rather than slaves who are beggars or servants who are employees. God has invested heavily in humanity, which includes you and me, since the time of Adam and Eve, and continues to do so today. He is looking for a Return On Investment (R.O.I.). God is an experienced investor and invests in all economic cycles. His investments are primarily in people, and His greatest investment was His Son, Jesus. One of the reasons that some Christians, and some churches and ministries, struggle with tithing is that they have a "poverty" or "beggar" spirit and mindset. Their focus is on them and their finite resources rather than God and His infinite resources. They practice tipping rather than tithing. This is dangerous since Romans 14: 23 says: "…everything that does not come from faith is sin."

It is beyond the scope of this writing to deal with this issue fully, but suffice it to say this is a serious and widespread problem in the church. The apostle Paul asked this insightful question: "He who did not spare his own Son, but gave him up for us all—how will he not also give us all things?" (Rom. 8:32). In other words, if we can trust God for our salvation since God did not withhold even His own Son, we can trust God with the things of lesser importance? Matthew 6:31-33 tells us that God is aware of our physical needs and that if we seek Him first, "..all these things shall be given to you as well."

☙❧☙❧☙❧☙

***Tithing is one way that God has
designed for His sons and daughters
to plant seeds and reap a harvest.***

☙❧☙❧☙❧☙

Tithing is part of planting seeds in good (fertile) soil, and so we have a responsibility to discern the type of soil we are sowing into, and also a right to expect a return on our investment as well, although that is not the primary reason or motivation to tithe, as we shall see.

In closing this section, we would be remiss if we failed to mention a few well- known Christian businessmen, who are known to have given 90% of their income to advance, support and further the work of the Kingdom of God on the earth while living on the remaining 10%. This short list for the so-called "reverse tithe" includes R.G. LeTourneau, J.C. Penney, Stanley Tam, and Peter J Daniels. There are no doubt others whose giving has been in secret but whose names are written in heaven.

Why Many Christians Don't Tithe?

In a report issued Feb. 8, 2010, by The Barna Group, Ltd. it was reported: "One measure of American generosity that has stayed relatively consistent – despite the economic turmoil – is the practice of tithing. This is the concept embraced by many Christians of giving ten percent (or more) of one's income. Overall, 7% of all adults reported donation levels equaling at least 10% of their income. The percentage of adults who tithe has remained constant since the beginning of the decade, falling in the 5% to 7% range.

Tithing levels, which could include both church and other charitable giving, were highest among evangelicals (24% of whom give at least 10%), non-mainline Protestants (13%), churchgoers (11%), and non-evangelical born-again Christians (10%). Those over the age of 45 (9%) were nearly twice as likely as those under age (5%) to tithe. Also, the study showed that income level was not correlated with tithing: just 9% of upscale adults gave at least one-tenth of their income, while 11% of the downscale set gave an equivalent proportion." (Permission granted by Barna Group Ltd. to cite this data.)

Apparently between 10% and 24% of US Christians are tithers; depending on which segment or category you belong to in the paragraph above. Probably the majority of those reading this book would fall into the largest category listed, Evangelicals, based on the definition of that term provided by Barna. That is a sobering statistic indeed and reinforces the need for this book. So despite the policies of some large Christian denominations with their annual tithe pledge commitment forms and Stewardship Committees, and the Mormon Church, which sanctions or disciplines non-tithe-paying members by barring them from being able to access or use church temples for important family ceremonies such as weddings or funerals, tithing percentages have remained about the same over the past decade in the US.

Such peer pressure and negative reinforcement tactics may affect behavior in the short term, but not the long term, and have no power to change the hearts of the givers or to teach the principle of honor. Some other Christian denominations actually require their member churches to send a tithe to the national church headquarters to support a large operations staff and international outreach programs.

The Unanswered Question Of Lordship:

"And I saw heaven opened, and behold a white horse, and he that sat upon him was called Faithful and true, and in righteousness doth he judge and make war. His eyes were as a fiame of fire, and on his head were many crowns; and he had a name written, that no man knew, but he himself. And he was clothed with a vesture dipped in blood: and his name is called The Word of God. And the armies which were in heaven followed him upon white horses, clothed in fine linen, white and clean. And out of his mouth goeth a sharp sword, that with it he should smite the nations: and he shall rule them with a rod of iron: and he treadeth the winepress of the fierceness and wrath of Almighty God. And he hath on his vesture and on his thigh a name written, KING OF KINGS, AND LORD OF LORDS." Revelation 19:11-16

The Church has begun what appears to be a "popular" upswing into the "Kingdom" mentality, lifestyle and language. However, one cannot have the Kingdom "mentality, lifestyle and language" without the important element of "Lordship." The term "Lord" is "Kurios" in Greek, meaning: Supremacy, supreme in authority, a controller and a position of respect. Webster defines "Lordship" as: The rank or dignity of a lord; the authority or territory of a lord. One may be a "King," but kings have to be strong in order to maintain dominion over their territory. "Lordship" is the strength of one's Kingdom attitude.

"And why call ye me, Lord, Lord, and do not the things which I say?" Luke 6:46 (KJV)

The Holy Spirit told me that one of the primary reasons why many Kingdom citizens struggle to tithe consistently is merely a shadow of a deeper spiritual struggle. The struggle to submit to Christ as "Lord." The larger body of Christ has accepted Christ as "Savior;" but they struggle to accept and honor Him as "Lord." The Body of Christ's lip service Lordship mentality has become a raging spiritual epidemic that has weakened the global Church. In Luke 6:46 Jesus told His apprentice apostles and his listening audience that it was redundant of them to call him "Lord" in one sentence and then refuse to do what He commanded them to do in the next. It is clear that in Jesus' mind that Lordship and total obedience are inseparable sides of the same coin. You cannot have one without the other.

The Online Thesaurus dictionary defines "Lordship" as follows: a person who has authority, control, or power over others; a master, chief, or ruler; a person who exercises authority from property rights; an owner of land, houses, etc. In Hebrew, the word "Lord" is "Adonai" which simply means "owner." So in the Hebrew context, Jesus is not your Lord, unless "He owns you and everything in your life." Are you failing the test of Lordship?

ఇ౨ఇ౨ఇ౨ఇ౨

Peer pressure and negative reinforcement
tactics may cause people to tithe in the
short term, but not in the long term.

ఇ౨ఇ౨ఇ౨ఇ౨

It is clear from the above definitions that the Body of Christ's struggle with the concept of the Lordship of Christ has mushroomed into a cornucopia of problems, including the current assault on tithing. In essence, most members of the Body of Christ do not really have a tithing problem; they have a Lordship problem. Tithing is merely a form of Kingdom tax or a seed of honor; that we are privileged to owe to the Kingdom of God in exchange for continued prosperity within the economy of the Kingdom? It is my humble experience that believers who have matured to the point where they no longer struggle with the Lordship of Christ over their life also discovered that tithing consistently was no longer an issue in their life. They quickly come to understand the fact that fighting over 10% is redundant when the hundred percent that they own already belongs to the Lord.

"And if any man ask you, Why do ye loose him? thus shall ye say unto him, Because the Lord hath need of him." Luke 19:31 (KJV)

I truly believe that the passage of Scripture above clearly lays down the premise for tithing for both the old and new Testaments. Jesus sent his disciples to the house of a certain man who owned a donkey. Jesus told his disciples that they would find this donkey tied to a pole in front of this man's house; He told them to lose the donkey and bring it to Jesus Christ. How could Jesus possibly lay claim to a donkey that belonged to another man; if he's not Lord of all?

However, since Jesus knew that He is Lord of all, and the creator of everything under the sun, He did not consider it robbery when He took the donkey away from its original owner. Jesus saw the donkey's human owner as a "steward" of an animal He created. Jesus told his disciples, that if the owner of the donkey asked them why they were taking his donkey, they were to simply say that the Lord had need of it. In Jesus' Royal mind, the declaration of His Lordship was sufficient reason for taking a donkey that belonged to another man. When we apply this principle to tithing it becomes quite clear that what we have in the body of Christ is not a tithing problem; it is a Lordship problem. Our "tithe" is like the donkey that we feel we own, only to discover that the Lord has need of it. Like the donkey, the Lord Jesus Christ needs our tithes to finance the advancement of His Kingdom in the earth.

Worrying About The Future:

"And why take ye thought for raiment? Consider the lilies of the field, how they grow; they toil not, neither do they spin." Matthew 6:27-29 (KJV)

"And which of you with taking thought can add to his stature one cubit? [26] If ye then be not able to do that thing which is least, why take ye thought for the rest? [27] Consider the lilies how they grow: they toil not, they spin not; and yet I say unto you, that Solomon in all his glory was not arrayed like one of these." Luke 12:25-27 (KJV)

There are people in the body of Christ who are chronic "worriers." They worry about everything. This section of the body of Christ is one of the reasons why many members of the body of Christ struggle with tithing consistently. It is very difficult to sow tithes of honor in a spiritual atmosphere that is governed by endless worries. This section of the body of Christ is an easy prey for those who claim that tithing is an Old Testament practice, which must never be imposed upon New Testament saints. These chronic "worriers" love this misguided view of tithing because it makes tithing one less thing that they have to worry about or deal with.

However, the Lord Jesus Christ was adamantly clear that worrying about tomorrow and what the future holds is futile and unmasks deep-seated disbelief in God and is His faithfulness to those who believe. Jesus also made it clear that worrying about tomorrow does not excuse us from obeying God and His word in the present. A life that is driven by worry is not God's ideal for His blood-washed children, but it does help us understand why many members of the body of Christ struggle in giving their tithes consistently.

A Fear-driven Perspective

"And he saith unto them, 'Why are ye fearful, O ye of little faith?' Then he arose, and rebuked the winds and the sea, and there was a great calm." Matthew 8:25-27 (KJV)

The saying that fear is a great motivator certainly has a lot of truth to it, but it is not a complete statement. In most cases "Fear" is the great "paralyzer" of mankind. Fear can be a great motivator when it is the kind of fear that can cause us to want to obey God or walk away from doing what is evil. However, the truth of the matter is that more often than not, Fear is more of a negative paralyzing force in the lives of so many of God's people. There are far too many members of the body of Christ governed by their fears than who are known by their faith. The Bible is very clear that the just shall live by faith and not by fear. But as the saying goes: It is easier said than done.

What we have in the body of Christ is not
a tithing problem; it is a Lordship problem.

ও৯৯৯৯৯

A friend of mine who goes by the stage name of Dr. Breakthrough defines "FEAR" as "False Evidence Appearing Real" and yet many members of the body of Christ seem to believe their fears more easily than they believe the word of God. This is "WHY" many members of the Body of Christ struggle to tithe consistently because the voice of their "FEAR" about letting "GO" of their tithe is louder than the voice of their faith or their desire to obey God.

Peter would never have become the first disciple of Christ to walk on water had he allowed his fear to choke his faith in the Christ who was bidding him to step out of the boat and walk on water.

Unfortunately, too many of God's people are ruled by their fears, especially their financial fears. These financial fears eventually become strongholds that choke their will or desire to honor God with their tithes. The problem with this scenario is that all fears that hinder men and women from obeying God are demonically engineered. All demonically engineered fears are designed to rob us of the blessing that God has in store for us. I wonder what would have happened to the widow of Sidon (1 Kings 17:8-15) had she allowed her fear of lack to stop her from sowing her last piece of bread into the life and ministry of the Prophet Elijah.

Little Faith

"Which when Jesus perceived, he said unto them, O ye of little faith, why reason ye among yourselves, because ye have brought no bread?" Matthew 16:7-9 (KJV)

Another reason "why" many followers of Christ struggle to give the tithe on a consistent basis is due to a spiritual disease that Jesus Christ called "Little Faith." Little Faith is faith that is easily choked and challenged by the circumstances surrounding God's people. It is the kind of faith that is barely enough to keep us saved. The only difference between followers of Christ with little faith and heathens is in the indwelling presence of the Holy Spirit. The difference pretty much ends there. Followers of Christ with "Little Faith" are controlled and governed by many of the same fleshly passions and fears that control the unsaved. It is not surprising that in a group of followers of Christ with "Little Faith," tithing consistently is quite a struggle. It takes great "faith and obedience" to tithe consistently.

❧❧❧❧❧❧

All demonically engineered fears are
designed to rob us of the blessing
that God has in store for us.

❧❧❧❧❧❧

The Green-eyed Monster Called Greed

We finally get to that devious green-eyed monster called greed. This green-eyed monster is responsible for much of the systemic corruption that permeates every crevice of both the political and business marketplace. This green-eyed monster invades the souls of men and women until it bends their heart to the idolatry called "covetousness." Covetousness is the "worship or love of money" that goes beyond the natural need for money to pay for life's necessities. It is a deep-seated love of money that literally challenges God's supreme authority over the human heart. This would explain why Jesus said that you cannot serve God and mammon. Mammon is the Greek name for this devious, the green-eyed monster that excites the engines of greed in the human heart.

"For the love of money is the root of all kinds of evil. And some people, craving money, have wandered from the true faith and pierced themselves with many sorrows." 1 Timothy 6:10 (New Living Translation)

The corridors of human history are plastered with the bloodstains of innocent people, who became collateral damage in the quest for "more money" by those who were in positions of authority. Kings went to war and sacrificed the lives of thousands of their royal soldiers just for the sake of increasing the royal treasury by a few more gold coins. Whenever this green-eyed monster possesses the soul of any human being, no amount of money is ever enough. There is always an underlying governing desire for more money. While this green-eyed monster rules the heart of a child of God tithing will always remain a huge struggle.

The Extravagant Lifestyle Of Prosperity Preachers

"These people always cause trouble. Their minds are corrupt, and they have turned their backs on the truth. To them, a show of godliness is just a way to become wealthy." Timothy 6:5 (New Living Translation)

One of the unfortunate reasons "why" many well-meaning people of faith have struggled to give their tithes consistently is due to the overly extravagant lifestyles of some proponents of the prosperity gospel. I want to make it very clear that I'm not against prosperity preachers and teachers and neither do I believe that there is any godly virtue to be found in being poverty-stricken. However, the above passage of scripture is also clear that godliness is not about monetary gain; it is about obedience to God.

I have personally witnessed the embarrassing and greed-driven extravagance of some so-called prosperity preachers. I know of a Bishop in Texas who had a church that had about 3000 members. His church building was valued at $4.5 million, but he was building himself a $7.0 million mansion to live in from monies collected aggressively from his faithful congregation. Many of his members were struggling financially but gave sacrificially towards the building of his mansion.

ఌఌఌ✲ఌఌ

__Mammon is the Greek name for the devious,__
__green-eyed monster that excites the engines__
__of greed in the human heart.__

ఌఌఌ✲ఌఌ

Unfortunately, this Bishop never got to finish building his luxurious mansion because the State of Texas sent him to prison for raping about 15 women by pouring "sleep-inducing drugs" in their cup of tea, when they came to him for counseling. Many of these women were from his congregation. His criminal trial was a public spectacle that brought shame to the cause of Christ and hurt the image of the church in general. Stories such as this are responsible for why many well-meaning believers refuse to give their tithes. Even though I empathize with many God-fearing people who have been put off from the practice of tithing because of the extravagant and flamboyant lifestyles of some prosperity preachers, the fact remains that tithing is a sacred New Testament form of worship.

Lack Of Financial Integrity

"And if you are untrustworthy about worldly wealth, who will trust you with the true riches of heaven?" Luke 16:11

Another reason why many God-fearing people of faith struggle to give their tithes consistently is due to the systemic lack of financial integrity that permeates the financial management systems of some congregations. I know pastors who treat their church finances as though it was their personal piggy bank. When members of their congregation pick up on this, it sends the wrong message about tithing. The truth of the matter is that the majority of church-going folk are not very wealthy. Many of them struggle to make ends meet, and as such when they tithe, they expect their money to be treated with the greatest level of financial integrity. I really believe that the more transparent and honorable the financial management systems of a church are, the more they will attract a growing number of faithful and consistent tithers. In my church (lovefestchurch.com) in the Phoenix-Metroplex, we have adopted an annual church business meeting, where our church's CPA and finance director give a full reporting to our congregation on how their monies were used during the year. This helps to break down the "veil of financial mistrust" that so many churchgoers have because of misappropriation of funds by some pastors.

False Doctrines About Tithing

"Then we will no longer be immature like children. We won't be tossed and blown about by every wind of new teaching. We will not be influenced when people try to trick us with lies so clever they sound like the truth. 15 Instead, we will speak the truth in love, growing in every way more and more like Christ, who is the head of his body, the church." Ephesians 4:14-15 (NLT)

I have already mentioned that when the Lord told me to write this book, he instructed me to Google the word tithing on the Internet. What I found was a mass proliferation of false doctrines on tithing. I've challenged many of these false doctrines in the second and third chapters of this writing. Nevertheless, the fact of the matter is that many of these false doctrines are responsible for why many well-meaning believers do not tithe consistently.

The Question Of Mounting Personal Debt

"Just as the rich rule the poor, so the borrower is a servant to the lender." Proverbs 22:7 (N L T)

Of all the reasons that we have examined thus far, the most compelling reason why many people of faith struggle to give their tithes consistently is due to mounting and overwhelming personal debt. Let's face it; the majority of the body of Christ is in dire distress when it comes to mounting personal debt. In America, for instance, the average American family is carrying $10,000 to $15,000 in credit card debt. With the high-interest rates charged by many credit card companies, the average American family feels very burdened by debt.

The unfortunate consequence of this mounting personal debt is the tendency for many people of faith to treat "tithing" as "additional debt." This attitude does little to inspire them to "sow their tithes of honor" into the Kingdom of the God who gave them everything they own. I believe that churches that are serious about empowering the members of their congregation to deal with their mounting personal debt through biblical financial stewardship principles are going to inevitably see a rise in the tithing numbers in their congregations. How churches help the members of their congregation deal with the issue of mounting personal debt is the key to stabilizing their churches. King Solomon the richest man, who has ever lived, tells us that the borrower is a slave to the lender, always.

A Question Of Obedience

"But Samuel replied, 'What is more pleasing to the Lord: your burnt offerings and sacrifices or your obedience to his voice? Listen! Obedience is better than sacrifice, and submission is better than offering the fat of rams. [23] Rebellion is as sinful as witchcraft, and stubbornness as bad as worshiping idols. So because you have rejected the command of the Lord, he has rejected you as king.'"
1 Samuel 15:22-23 (NLT)

One of the primary reasons why many people of faith struggle with giving their tithes consistently is due to the lack of obedience to God's Word and His delegated authority that is becoming an epidemic in many congregations across the nations of the world, especially in the liberal-minded Western world. Thankfully, the Bible is very clear that obedience is better than sacrifice. This writing will show that tithing is an integral part of the expression of faith of Kingdom citizens, both in the Old and New Testaments. Paul the Apostle in the book of Hebrews (Chapter 7) makes it fairly clear that there is a priesthood in the New Testament that receives the tithes of God's people, just like there was a priesthood (Levites) that received the tithes of God's people in the Old Testament. Unfortunately, the engines of disobedience are so powerful and prevalent in many of God's people. The enemy continues to rob many followers of Christ of the covenant blessings of the tithe, while simultaneously hindering the financial stability of many congregations.

Excessive Use Of The Malachi Tithing Model

"You are under a curse, for your whole nation has been cheating me. [10] Bring all the tithes into the storehouse so there will be enough food in my Temple. If you do," says the Lord of Heaven's Armies, *"I will open the windows of heaven for you. I will pour out a blessing so great you won't have enough room to take it in! Try it! Put me to the test!"* Malachi 3:9-10 (NLT)

One of the reasons "why" many born-again believers struggle to give their tithes consistently is due to the excessive use of the Malachi 3 tithing system by most pastors in their endeavor to exact tithes from the members of their local church. Several well-meaning, born-again believers have been told so many times from the pulpit that they are cursed if they do not tithe. Many of them have told me that they have become numb to the impact of this over-used expression. Some of them told me, *"Dr. Myles, why bother if I'm already cursed because I failed to pay my tithes on several occasions in my walk of faith?"*

However, it is serious students of the Word that have posed the most difficult challenge to the tithing question. "Dr. Myles, why do preachers tell us that we are cursed with a curse if we do not give our tithes; when Galatians 3:13 is very clear that Jesus Christ became a curse for us on the cross? Ephesians 1:3 also says, "Blessed be the God and Father of our Lord Jesus Christ who has already blessed us with every spiritual blessing in heavenly places. We are either cursed, or Christ has removed the "curse" on the cross. So which is which?" Whenever I am asked this important theological question, my answer is always in the affirmative.

❧❧❧❧❧❧❧

*Many people of faith struggle to give their
tithes consistently is due to mounting
and overwhelming personal debt.*

❧❧❧❧❧❧❧

Without a doubt, Christ became a curse for us on the cross so that the blessing of Abraham would come upon the Gentiles. Even though tithing is important, biblical and honorable, it cannot be placed on the same level as the atoning blood of Jesus Christ. The apostle Paul is very clear in the book of Galatians that the shed blood of Jesus Christ atoned for the curse of the law. The curse described in Malachi 3:9 is part of the curse of the law.

But the real reason "why" most pastors rely heavily on Malachi 3 when teaching on tithing is because, for many of them, Malachi 3 seems to be the best portion of Scripture, that really describes the importance of tithing to the local church. As a pastor of a thriving church, I know the importance of tithing to sustaining the local ministry expression that most churches are involved in. However, my purpose for writing this book is to show well-meaning pastors a more excellent way of exacting the tithe from New Testament believers without relying on Malachi 3.

I can't afford it

Unfortunately, many church-goers have a poverty mindset and spirit. They are still living as slaves rather than sons, and are led by fear rather than faith. Many in the church are employees rather than entrepreneurs, consumers rather than producers. Many in the church live from paycheck to paycheck, barely irking out an existence and in debt up to their eyeballs, when God desires that we have multiple streams of income. "Give a serving to seven, and also to eight,

---

"For you do not know what evil will be on the earth. ³ If the clouds are full of rain, They empty themselves upon the earth; And if a tree falls to the south or the north, In the place where the tree falls, there it shall lie. ⁴ He who observes the wind will not sow, and he

who regards the clouds will not reap. [5] As you do not know what is the way of the [a] wind, Or how the bones grow in the womb of her who is with child, So you do not know the works of God who makes everything. [6] In the morning sow your seed, and in the evening do not withhold your hand; For you do not know which will prosper, Either this or that, Or whether both alike will be good (Ecc. 11:2-6)."

My Giving is so Small: It Won't Make a Difference

Then they are those who do not participate in tithing because they don't believe their giving actually makes a difference. They say, "What I have to give is so small it won't make a difference. God doesn't need or won't miss my little pittance." Unfortunately, this is shame-based thinking. "He is that faithful in little will be ruler over much." (Matt. 25:23) "For if the willingness is there, the gift is acceptable according to what one has, not according to he does not have (2 Cor. 8:12)."

There is too much uncertainty in the world

Then they are those who do not participate in tithing because they have paralysis by analysis. They say, "There is too much uncertainty in the world, politics, economy, job market, my business, my marriage, etc. to tithe. I need to hoard and save for a rainy day." Again, this is Fear-based thinking and futile, fatalistic human reasoning. 2 Cor. 10:3-5 says to take captive such thoughts since they are opposed to the knowledge of Christ. God holds our future, and we came here on Earth to finish a "work" that is already "finished" in heaven. So we have nothing to fear.

I am the only one who can steward my tithe!

Then they are those who do not participate in tithing because they don't trust giving their "tithes" to their local church, so they distribute it as they see it fit. They say, "Since God gave me the money I have, I should be the one to steward my tithe. Since God obviously trusts me, why should I let someone else manage my tithe?." This is Pride-based thinking. This is a "strong delusion" fueled by a spirit of control and manipulation. These people say that the "storehouse" is the world, or a charity or nonprofit, not the local church. Nothing could be further from the truth. This is just another deception from Satan. More will be said on this later.

Final Analysis

In the final analysis, this book of "WHY" only serves to show us that even though the reasons that many people of faith struggle with tithing consistently are understandable on a human level, they are nothing more than a convergence of demonic technologies that are designed to rob us of the covenantal blessings invoked by the tithe. In the final analysis, "Obedience is better than sacrifice (1 Sam 15:22)." Interestingly enough, all of the proponents who believe that tithing is not applicable to New Testament believers have one thing in common. Very few of them if any have a burning desire to give God more than ten percent of their income, even though they profess that everything they own belongs to the Lord.

తుళిళిళిళ

*Why bother tithing if I'm already cursed because
I failed to pay my tithes on several occasions.*
తుళిళిళిళ

Many of them have argued passionately with me that "tithing" is legalistic and that New Testament believers are free to give God any percentage that He wants them to give because everything they own belongs to God 100%. What never ceases to amaze me is how God somehow leads these people, collectively, to give Him and His Kingdom as little of their resources as possible. The God who gave us 100% of His only begotten Son, somehow spares them from giving sacrificially. This is when I concluded that there is a diabolical conspiracy by demonic and religious spirits against the biblical practice of tithing in the body of Christ. Thankfully, this book will unmask this diabolical conspiracy that is designed to rob Kingdom citizens of the benefits and privileges of tithing.

LIFE APPLICATION SECTION

Point to Ponder

There is a diabolical conspiracy of demonic powers against the biblical practice of tithing in the body of Christ.

Memory Verse

He who observes the wind will not sow, and he who regards the clouds will not reap. 5 As you do not know what is the way of the [a] wind, Or how the bones grow in the womb of her who is with child, So you do not know the works of God who makes everything. Ecclesiastes 11:4-6

Reflections ReRe

1. Why is Greed a critical factor as to why many people of faith struggle to give their tithes consistently?

_____

_____

_____

_____

2. Why did God create or ordain the tithe?"

_____

_____

_____

_____

3. Most born again believers struggle to accept Christ's Lordship, even though they easily embrace Him as Savior, why is this so?

_____

_____

_____

_____

Chapter Seven

Tithes of Honor: Why Abraham Tithed

"And blessed be God Most High, who has defeated your enemies for you." Then Abram gave Melchizedek a tenth of all the goods he had recovered. Genesis 14:20

Why did Abraham tithe into Melchizedek? Much of the tithing that is done today in most churches lacks Abraham's primary and inherent motivation. Abraham was so moved by this man's spiritual stature and divine royalty that he did something that was customary but not foreign to the people of the ancient world. Abraham's response to Melchizedek was ignited by his personal sense of awe and by the prevailing cultural protocol of his era. People of the ancient world never went to see a "King" without a "gift or endowment" to honor the King with. In Abraham's eyes, Melchizedek was the greatest and most glorious King that he had ever met. Out of this "deep sense of honor and personal awe," Abraham, the father of the faithful, gave "his first tithes into the priestly Order of Melchizedek," thereby establishing a prophetic tithing model for all his spiritual descendants.

Tithing to Advance the Kingdom

Abraham tithed into the royal priesthood of Melchizedek (the king-priest). Simply put, Abraham gave tithes to a "King" and not just to a "priest." Since every "King" has a "Kingdom," it is safe to assume that Abraham's tithes were used to support and advance the "Kingdom." Everything that is given to a "King" becomes part of his royal estate. This means then that the "Abrahamic tithing model" is a "Kingdom-driven and Kingdom-minded tithing model." This is why it is the highest form and level of tithing mentioned in the Scriptures. Under the Levitical priesthood, "tithes" were given to "support the priesthood" (the clergy), whereas, under the Order of Melchizedek, tithes are given to "support and sustain" the advancement of God's Kingdom here on earth.

> *And this gospel of the kingdom will be preached in all the world as a witness to all the nations, and then the end will come.*
> Matthew 24:14

Since Abraham's tithes were employed to advance a "Kingdom," and Abraham is referred to as the "father of faith" and the "father of us all" (Rom. 4:1-25; Gal. 3:6-9), it is quite erroneous and misleading for us to say that there is no requirement for tithing in the New Testament, especially considering the fact that New Testament living has a greater emphasis on advancing God's Kingdom here on earth than was ever emphasized under the Old Testament. Furthermore, Abraham did not tithe into Melchizedek because he felt like Melchizedek could use the money. Abraham knew that there was nothing in his possession that could pay for the services of such a great King. Abraham's motivation for tithing and the reasons why he tithed are sadly missing in much of today's tithing practices. This is why it's imperative that we rediscover this "Lost Key," which is tithing according to the Order of Melchizedek.

જીજીજીજી

Abraham's tithes were used to support and advance the "Kingdom."

જીજીજીજી

Tithes of Honor

"He lifts the poor from the dust and the needy from the garbage dump. He sets them among princes, placing them in seats of honor. For all the earth is the Lord's, and he has set the world in order."
1 Samuel 2:8

There is nothing more powerful and life-giving than the bestowment of honor upon those for whom honor is due. The primary being who deserves to be honored by all of His creation is "God." Honor is one of the most important principles of the Kingdom of God. It is the cornerstone of kingdom living; without it, kingdoms go into a state of decline. No spiritual culture can ever be referred to as a "Kingdom culture" which does not have this "principle of honor" deeply embedded in it. "Honor" quickly establishes itself as a divine life-giving principle whenever it is instituted into any relationship. Marriages, governments, friendships, covenants, and business relationships flourish whenever the principle of honor is engrafted into them.

"Honor your father and your mother, that your days may be long upon the land which the LORD your God is giving you."
Exodus 20:12

"Jesus replied, And why do you break the command of God for the sake of your tradition? ⁴ For God said, 'Honor your father and mother' and 'Anyone who curses his father or mother must be put to death.' ⁵ But you say that if a man says to his father or mother, 'Whatever help you might otherwise have received from me is a gift devoted to God.'" Matthew 15:3-5

In the synoptic gospels, Jesus Christ went as far as establishing the "spiritual connection" between "honor" and "material prosperity and long life." Jesus made it very clear that "children" who "honor" their "parents" are guaranteed a long and prosperous life. Children who did not honor their parents were deserving of death. Whoa! What an incredible promise from the mouth of God! It is the reason I honor my natural and spiritual parents. Unfortunately for many of us, especially those of us who live in morally liberal nations like the United States of America, the "principle of honor" is foreign to our culture. The culture-war between Judaic-Christian values and secular liberalism has taken its toll. We live in a nation where insulting governing authorities and undermining spiritual leaders is commonplace. It is quite difficult to show people (including Christians) the critical importance of the "principle of honor" to the survival of any civilization. The principle of honor is so powerful, it incites God to honor those who honor Him.

> *"Whoso keepeth the fig-tree shall eat the fruit thereof, And he that regardeth his master shall be honored."* Proverbs 27:18 (ASV)

Abraham lived in a Kingdom culture that understood the critical importance of bestowing honor on governing authorities and those to whom honor is due. Abraham understood that the quickest way to unleash the "favor and blessing" of a King is to approach him from a position of heartfelt honor. The "principle of honor" was the governing principle behind Abraham's motivation for tithing into Melchizedek the divine King-priest. This principle of honor is sadly missing in much of the technology of tithing in the Body of Christ.

"Honor" quickly establishes itself as a divine life-giving principle whenever it is instituted into any relationship.

Honor Versus Fear Based Tithing!

One of the main reasons why the Malachi 3:8-12 tithing model is so popular is that it "frightens Christians and Kingdom citizens into tithing."

Psychologists will quickly tell you that "fear" is a great motivator. However, the Bible is clear that "fear" as a motivator appeals to our lower (carnal) nature whereas "honor" appeals to our higher (divine) nature.

I really believe that God will use this book to restore the "principle of honor" in the Church's tithing model. Many Kingdom citizens (including most Christians) are going to discover how to give "tithes of honor" to advance the Kingdom of God here on earth. They will quickly discover that honor is a greater motivator than fear and God will also respond by honoring them for honoring Him. What would motivate a rookie basketball or football player to use his signing-bonus money to build a magnificent home for his single mother? The answer is "honor."

Honor is truly the greatest and highest motivator for giving to those in authority over us, who have served us well. Churches that are currently using the spiritual technology of tithing that is found in this book have told me that the total amount of tithing in their church has increased dramatically. It did not surprise me at all. I knew that once they established a "spiritual culture of honor" around tithing, their tithes would inevitably go up. It is my prayer that in the near future, all tithing in the global Church will be done this way.

๛๖๏๖๛๖๏

The principle of honor is sadly missing
in much of the technology of
tithing in the Body of Christ.

๛๖๏๖๛๖๏

Seven Reasons to Give to a King

So the King will greatly desire your beauty; because He is your Lord, worship Him.[12] And the daughter of Tyre will come with a gift; The rich among the people will seek your favor. Psalm 45:11-12

Dr. Myles Munroe in his best-selling book Kingdom Principles lists seven reasons why citizens of a kingdom give to a reigning King. I have taken the liberty to quote him verbatim on these seven reasons so that we can gain a greater understanding as to why and how Abraham tithed into Melchizedek. Please remember that Melchizedek was both the King of heavenly Jerusalem, as well as a Priest of God Most High.

- "Royal protocol requires that a gift must be presented when visiting a king. This is why the queen of Sheba brought such lavish gifts to King Solomon even though he was richer than she was. It was royal protocol. He would have done the same had he visited her.
- The gift must be fitting for the king. Worse than approaching a king with no gift is to bring a gift unworthy of him. An inappropriate or inadequate gift amounts to an insult to the king. It shows that the giver does not properly respect the king or his authority.
- The gift reveals our value of "worth-ship" of the king. The quality of what we offer the King and the attitude with which we offer it reveals much more than our words do of the value or worthiness we attach to Him.
- Worship demands a gift and giving is worship. "Worth-ship" is where we get "worship." To worship a King means to ascribe worth or worthiness to Him. And as we have already seen, that always involves bringing Him a gift. There is no genuine worship without gift giving. But giving is itself an act of worship, and worship is always fitting for the King. The Magi who saw his star in the east understood this, which is why they brought gifts when they came to find Him.
- Giving to a king attracts his favor. Kings are attracted to people who give with a willing and grateful spirit. Like anyone else, a king likes to know he is loved and appreciated. The King of Heaven is the same way. The Giver is attracted to the giver and extends His favor. Gifts open doors to blessings, opportunities, and prosperity.
- Giving to a king acknowledges his ownership of everything. Remember kings are lords; they own everything in their domain. So giving to a king is simply returning to him what is already his. This is why in the Kingdom of Heaven we are always stewards and never owners.

- Giving to a king is Thanksgiving. One of the best ways to express gratitude is with a gift. Gratitude expressed is in itself a gift. (*Kingdom Principles* by Dr. Myles Munroe, pgs. 211-213)

LIFE APPLICATION SECTION

Point to Ponder:

When God is involved with the affairs of our human life, the devil will also hasten to intercept the course of our lives to see if he can derail us from pursuing our spiritual purpose.

Memory Verse

"He lifts the poor from the dust and the needy from the garbage dump. He sets them among princes, placing them in seats of honor. For all the earth is the Lord's, and he has set the world in order." 1 Samuel 2:8

Reflections

1. Why is it important to bring a gift when you come before the King of kings?

   _____

   _____

   _____

   _____

2. What was Abraham's mindset when he tithed into the priestly Order of Melchizedek?

   _____

   _____

   _____

   _____

3. What did Melchizedek give to Abraham in exchange for his tithes of honor?

   _____

   _____

   _____

   _____

Chapter Eight

Tithing a Righteous Trading Floor

And blessed be God Most High, who has defeated your enemies for you." Then Abram gave Melchizedek a tenth of all the goods he had recovered. Genesis 14:20 (NLT)

Tithing is a righteous trading floor or platform. I want this statement to sink into your spirit and subconscious mind as deeply as humanly possible. *It's important to understand from the onset that "all kingdoms" or nations for that matter advance and flourish through "Trading."* This explains why world history is replete with stories of ferocious wars between kingdoms or nations over control of strategic trade routes or outposts. It will be difficult for us to truly appreciate the importance of the "Kingdom principle of tithing" if we fail to grasp the critical importance of "trading in the spirit world." One of the best books on the importance of trading floors in the spirit world is a book by Judy Coventry called "The Trading Floors." I encourage you to get this book on Amazon or marketplacebible.com.

Defining a Trading Floor

By definition "Trading" is defined as follows:

1. The act or process of buying, selling, or exchanging commodities, at either wholesale or retail, within a country or between countries:
2. The act of buying, selling, or exchanging stocks, bonds, or currency:
3. A purchase or sale; business deal or transaction.
4. Whereas a **Trading floor** is the area in a bank or stock exchange where securities are traded.

Trading in the Spirit

Again, the devil took Him up on an exceedingly high mountain, and showed Him all the kingdoms of the world and their glory. [9] *And he said to Him, "All these things I will give You if You will fall down and worship me." Matthew 4:8-9* (NKJV)

Since all kingdoms survive, expand and thrive through trading, "Trading in the spirit" becomes one of the most important spiritual activities a human being can ever participate in. In keeping with the principle that all kingdoms advance through trade. Like a mafia godfather Satan offered Jesus a deal (trade) he failed he couldn't resist. Satan asked Jesus to bow down and worship him in exchange for becoming Satan's landlord over all the kingdoms of this world. Had Jesus accepted this "unrighteous trade" He would have become subordinate to the devil. He would have also failed to accomplish His God given assignment as the savior of the world and the rest of us would still be prisoners of sin and death. Thankfully for all of us, Jesus chose wisely.

"Once when Jacob was cooking some stew, Esau came in from the open country, famished. He said to Jacob, 'Quick, let me have some of that red stew! I'm famished!' (That is why he was also called Edom.) Jacob replied, 'First sell me your birthright.' 'Look, I am about to die,' Esau said. 'What good is the birthright to me?' But Jacob said, 'Swear to me first.' So he swore an oath to him, selling his birthright to Jacob. Then Jacob gave Esau some bread and

some lentil stew. He ate and drank, and then got up and left. So Esau despised his birthright." Genesis 27:29-34 (NKJV)

On the other hand Esau made a "bad or unrighteous trade" when he sold his God given birthright for a bowl of porridge. Later on, when he realized what he had done, he tried to undo his bad trade. Unfortunately he found no place of repentance; even though he sought to reverse what he had done with tears of regret. In this sense Esau's story is the best example of the difference between a righteous and an unrighteous trade. A righteous trade causes us to trade away the "carnal things of this world" for the "pricelessly spiritual." An unrighteous trade is the exact opposite. *There is ample biblical evidence that unrighteous trades are usually followed by intense times of pain and regret.* Judas Iscariot traded his divinely orchestrated apostleship for 30 pieces of "tainted silver." His unrighteous trade was so catastrophic he did not live long enough to enjoy the rewards of his betrayal.

"Men and brethren, this Scripture had to be fulfilled, which the Holy Spirit spoke before by the mouth of David concerning Judas, who became a guide to those who arrested Jesus; 17 for he was numbered with us and obtained a part in this ministry."18 (Now this man purchased a field with the]wages of iniquity; and falling headlong, he burst open in the middle and all his entrails gushed out. 19 And it became known to all those dwelling in Jerusalem; so that field is called in their own language, Akel Dama, that is, Field of Blood.) Acts 1:16-19 (NKJV)

The bible actually shows us that Satan's fall from his exalted position, as a glorious Archangel was due to his "trafficking" in unrighteous trade. Lucifer was anointed and appointed to lead all the angels in heaven in the passionate worship of God. Instead he traded this glorious position for his desire to be like God. In other words he started trading in pride, instead of trading in the true worship of God. His unrighteous trade caused him and one third of the angels he deceived to be expelled from the heavenly kingdom. *"By the abundance of your trading You became*

84

filled with violence within, and you sinned; Therefore I cast you as a profane thing out of the mountain of God; And I destroyed you, O covering cherub, From the midst of the fiery stones (Ezekiel 28:16). Since this historic fall, Satan's number one assignment is to deceive God's children into participating in unrighteous trade. Using the vehicle of unrighteous trade, the devil managed to deceive Adam and Eve into trading away their God given position of dominion in the Garden of Eden for the "forbidden fruit," which was supposed to make them like God.

ৡ৾৽৾ঌ৾৽৾ঌ৾

Unrighteous trade caused Lucifer and one third of the angels he deceived to be expelled from the heavenly kingdom.

ৡ৾৽৾ঌ৾৽৾ঌ৾

You might be asking, Dr. Myles what has trading got to do with tithing? The answer is "everything." **God established tithing in order to give His people a "righteous trading platform" where we can 'exchange our carnal things (money) for "things" (true riches) that money cannot buy."** When we withhold our tithes we are robbing ourselves of the opportunity to "spiritually trade" for the priceless "things" that God's kingdom offers. If most Christians knew this they would fall over each other to give God their tithes of honor. Perhaps there is no spiritual or natural venue that lends itself to "trading" like the marketplace. Today's marketplace is a congregate mix of righteous and unrighteous trades. Many people in business have sold their souls to the devil for an extra buck. Hell is full of such "sorry" tormented souls who sold their God-given birthright for a bowl of porridge during their earthly pilgrimage.

ৡ৾৽৾ঌ৾৽৾ঌ৾

Tithing into the priesthood of Melchizedek preserved Abram from trading on the unrighteous trading floor of the king of Sodom.

ৡ৾৽৾ঌ৾৽৾ঌ৾

Tithing into the eternal priesthood of Melchizedek preserved Abram from trading on the unrighteous trading floor presented by the king of Sodom, who came ready to trade with Abram. He unsuccessfully tried to lure Abraham into trading for the "perishable goods" of this world in exchange for the priceless souls of men; Abram had recovered in battle! Fortunately the divine interception, Abraham had received moments earlier through Melchizedek's priesthood saved the day! Abraham's tithes of honor into Melchizedek's priesthood were such a transformational righteous trade; his tithes secured the "future priesthood" of his grandson Levi, who was still in the loins of Abraham when Melchizedek met him. *I just want you to remember that each time you honor God with your "tithes" you are securing the future posterity of your unborn descendants.*

LIFE APPLICATION SECTION

Point to Ponder:

Tithing is one of the powerful righteous trading floors or platforms.

Memory Verse:

"By the abundance of your trading You became filled with violence within, and you sinned; Therefore I cast you as a profane thing out of the mountain of God; And I destroyed you, O covering cherub, From the midst of the fiery stones. Ezekiel 28:16 (NKJV)

Questions to Consider:

1. What is an unrighteous trade?

_____

_____

_____

_____

2. How does trading advance kingdoms?

_____

_____

_____

_____

3. Why did Melchizedek introduce tithing in the Marketplace?

_____

_____

_____

_____

Chapter Nine

What Are You Tithing For?

"And blessed be God Most High, who has defeated your enemies for you. Then Abram gave Melchizedek a tenth of all the goods he had recovered." Genesis 14:20

It's my humble opinion that one of the most important questions in this entire book is the title of this chapter. "What are you tithing for?" Unfortunately, much of the teaching on tithing compels God's people to tithe for the acquisition of more money. This is very sad because, in the economy of the Kingdom, "money" is the lost asset in God's kingdom. Why? Precisely because "money" is not a creation of God. It is the creation of fallen man after he lost access to the original Edenic economy after Adam and Eve fell from grace.

The most important thing I can tell you in this book is "stop tithing for money!" You don't need tithing to make money. Life is full of billionaires and multimillionaires who made their money without giving or paying tithes. I know my statement is shocking to many of you, who were told by well-meaning but misguided pastors that "acquiring more money" is the highest benefit of tithing. As a child of God while you don't need tithing to make money, you will ***need tithing to protect yourself and your money*** from the onslaught of demonic powers and technologies, that hate to see Christians prospering in today's Marketplace.

Stop Tithing for Money!

Therefore if you have not been faithful in the unrighteous mammon,
who will commit to your trust the true riches? Luke 16:11

Let's be honest for a second. How many of you have been tithing faithfully and yet your bank account is still screaming help? You are not yet a millionaire, and many of you may never become one. Many faithful "tithers" are angry because they feel like the church lied to them. Unfortunately, they arrived at the wrong conclusion; which is that "tithing does not work." Nothing could be further from the truth. But if you have been conditioned to "tithe for money," I totally understand their deep-seated frustration when they don't see the money they were promised in their bank account. However, it's my prayer that this book will be the end of you "tithing for money." We must stop insulting God in our tithing modality by stopping to "tithe" for the lowest asset that the Kingdom of God has to offer. When the Holy Spirit was showing me the fallacy of tithing for money, He showed me something about Abraham that I had never seen before.

"Francis, have you ever wondered why I waited until Abraham was very rich in gold and silver before I introduced him to the Kingdom principle of tithing?" This question from the LORD stunned me. I had never seen this important fact. Suddenly I was extremely interested in the LORD's answer. I did not have to wait long. "Francis, I waited because I did not want Abraham to connect tithing to the acquisition of more money. I introduced Abraham to tithing to give him access to "things" that money cannot buy." My spirit was resonating with unfeigned excitement. I found myself saying, "Wow!" Then the LORD placed the icing on the cake. "Francis tell my people that "money" will always follow them as a by-product of tithing correctly and for the right reasons. But getting more money must never be the primary objective of any godly tithing system." My dear friends, I am happy to report that my wife and I no longer tithe for money. We tithe for "things or divine products" money cannot buy. In this chapter, I will show you what to tithe for.

ഏഏഏഏഏ
Unfortunately, much of the teaching on
tithing compels God's people to tithe
for the acquisition of more money.
ഏഏഏഏഏ

Tithing for Divine Interception

And the king of Sodom went out to meet him at the Valley of Shaveh (that is, the King's Valley), after his return from the defeat of Chedorlaomer and the kings who were with him. Then Melchizedek king of Salem brought out bread and wine; he was the priest of God Most High. And he blessed him and said: "Blessed be Abram of God Most High, Possessor of heaven and earth; And blessed be God Most High, Who has delivered your enemies into your hand." And he gave him a tithe of all. Genesis 14:17-20

"Simon, Simon, Satan has asked to sift each of you like wheat. But I have pleaded in prayer for you, Simon, that your faith should not fail. So when you have repented and turned to me again, strengthen your brothers." Luke 22:31-32 (NLT)

When Abraham gave his first tithe, he gave it to "honor a man who was a Priest of God Most High." Abraham recognized the fact that this man had been raised by God to "intercept his life with the blessing of God." Melchizedek appeared in Abram's life at a very critical and strategic time in his life. Abraham was on a collision cause with one of the most diabolical demonic systems (king of Sodom). Fortunately for Abram, Melchizedek appeared and stood between Abram and the king of Sodom. Melchizedek actually "refereed" the encounter between Abram and the king of Sodom, tilting the results of the encounter in Abraham's favor. I know of a brother in Tulsa, Oklahoma who told by a prophet that God wanted him to audit his company within 90 days. At the time of the prophecy, he had $50 Million just sitting in the Bank. Unfortunately, two of his business partners convinced not to audit his company in the 90-day window declared by the prophet. This mistake would prove fatal to his well-accumulated wealth. About four months later, the FBI (Federal Bureau of Investigations) agents entered his business premises. They took control of his company computers and froze any access he had previously to the $50 Million just sitting in the Bank. When I met this man, all the money was gone, and he had also lost his lucrative company. It was discovered that his two business partners who did not want him to audit the company where the ones who practicing securities fraud and they were also planning a hostile take over of his company. He cried bitterly to me and told me, "Why wasn't I taught to tithe for the divine interception instead of tithing for money? I wouldn't be in this mess had I allowed the Holy Spirit to intercept like He wanted to."

According to Roget's Dictionary, Intercept means:

- *To take, seize or halt (someone or something on the way from some place to another); cut off from an intended destination: to intercept a messenger.*
- *To destroy or disperse (enemy aircraft or a missile or missiles) in the air on the way to a target.*
- *To stop or interrupt the course, progress or transmission of*

I hope that you are as excited as I am about the far-reaching spiritual implications of what it means for you and I to be intercepted by God before a demonic nuclear missile overruns us. Divine interception means that God apprehends us before the enemy can get to us! After Abram soundly defeated the kings from the East that had plundered Sodom, news of his resounding victory reached the ears of the king of Sodom. The king of Sodom quickly informed the keeper of his royal chariots to mount his horses because they were going to intercept Abram on his return. The king of Sodom put on his royal garments and fumed himself in the oils and fragrances which were offered in worship to his was in a demonic hurry to intercept Abram, but he was too late.

❧❧❧❧❧❧❧

I introduced Abraham to tithing to give him
access to "things" that money cannot buy."

❧❧❧❧❧❧❧

Before the king of Sodom got to him, Abraham was divine intercepted by Melchizedek's priesthood. Melchizedek offered Abram life elements from eternity "bread and wine" that completely changed in the internal configurations of Abram's life. By the time the king of Sodom showed up and tried to entice Abraham into participating in "unrighteous trade," Abraham was no longer interested in such deals. Consequently, whatever the devil had been planning to entrap with him had he participated in "unrighteous trade," was completely thwarted. Divine interception is one of the highest benefits of tithing under the Order of Melchizedek. Bill Gates or Oprah Winfrey may never "tithe" for money because they have too much of it. However, I am sure both of them would tithe for the release of the technology of divine interception in their life. What good is having billions of dollars in your account if you jump into a plane that is doomed to crash? Money doesn't mean much when you are dead! I always say that the most dangerous bullets in your life are the ones you don't see coming. This is were "divine interception" comes in, to save you from the bullets you don't see coming for you.

Tithing for Fulfillment of Divine Promises

And he blessed him and said: "Blessed be Abram of God Most High, Possessor of heaven and earth; And blessed be God Most High, Who has delivered your enemies into your hand." And he gave him a tithe of all. Genesis 14:19-20

But he whose genealogy is not derived from them received tithes from Abraham and blessed him who had the promises. Now beyond all contradiction, the lesser is blessed by, the better. Hebrews 7:6-7

How many of us are nurturing promises from God that are yet to be realized? Doesn't the bible say, "hope differed makes the heart sick?' As I travel across the nations, I see the frustration of "unfulfilled prophecies" on the faces of many members of the body of Christ. Ask yourself the question, "how radically different would your life be if everything God promised you came to pass in your lifetime?" When Abraham gave "tithes," he tithed into a man of God who had the "spiritual stature" to move Abraham into his spiritual destiny. This lofty priest and heavenly man, Melchizedek, became Abraham's "power center" for the divine fulfillment of the promises of God that he had been holding to.

The writer of Hebrews clearly shows us that Abraham's tithing into the priesthood of Melchizedek accelerated the divine fulfillment of his God-given promises. Hebrews 7:6 says, Melchizedek blessed he (Abraham) who had the promises! The "tithes" of Abraham became the fuel or trigger for the actualization of promises from God that he had been waiting on; chief among them is becoming the father of many nations. I believe as you embrace tithing under the Order of Melchizedek, divine promises made will soon become divine promises fulfilled.

Tithing for Heavenly Bread and Wine

Then Melchizedek king of Salem brought out bread and wine; he was the priest of God Most High. And he blessed him and said: "Blessed be Abram of God Most High, Possessor of heaven and earth; And blessed be God Most High, Who has delivered your enemies into your hand." And he gave him a tithe of all. Genesis 14:18-20

Melchizedek, the king of righteousness and peace who was also a priest of God Most high gave Abram, "heavenly bread and wine." These two elements were not natural they were spiritual elements from eternity containing God's divine nature. In biblical prophetic language "Bread" represents "Jesus' life and also deliverance from demons." Bread also represents the "doctrine of the Kingdom of God," whereas "Wine" represents the "Spirit of the Kingdom of God or the spirit of revelation!" How much money can you place on deliverance from demons or from evil?

⋙⋘⋙⋘⋙⋘
I see the frustration of "unfulfilled prophecies"
on the faces of many members of the body of Christ.
⋙⋘⋙⋘⋙⋘

Every time I give my tithes under the Order of Melchizedek I normally project them towards the unending manifestation of "deliverance and revelation." We live in an information age and those who are masters of it, are the financial and political power centers of this world. However, God is the only one who can produce the "product" known as "revelation." Through "revelation" God is giving His people across the nations of the world, the knowledge of witty inventions, innovation as well as "money-making ideas." I am convinced that any person who is rich in divine revelation will never be poor. This is why I am teaching Kingdom citizens all over the world to tithe for "revelation." Revelation is a thousand times more valuable than money. So when you begin to get overwhelmed by "revelation" just know that the "tithe" is working for you, whether there is money in your bank account or not. In my church we never "collect tithes of honor" from God's people, without taking Holy Communion. This is because we want our people to always remember that they are "tithing" into the "finished work of Christ."

Tithing Because You are Already Blessed

And he blessed him and said: "Blessed be Abram of God Most High, Possessor of heaven and earth; And blessed be God Most High, Who has delivered your enemies into your hand." And he gave him a tithe of all. Genesis 14:19-20

One of the most unfortunate by-products of the church's usage of the Malachi 3 tithing system is that it has created a generation of God's children who are always "tithing to be blessed." Many of them have been told a countless times that "if you don't tithe you are cursed with a curse." However, this pronouncement is both erroneous and theologically incorrect. This statement by Pastors while exacting tithes from New Testament believers who under the covenant of grace, flies in the face of Ephesians 1:3. Saint Paul declares, "Blessed God and father of our Lord Jesus Christ, who has already blessed us with every spiritual blessing in Christ."

This verse from the book of Ephesians can't be anymore clear than it is. God has already blessed us with every spiritual blessing in Christ." However, under the Malachi 3 tithing system, the saints go from "being blessed to being cursed" depending upon whether they tithed or not. Tithing is an important Kingdom principle that all children of God should actively participate in. But threatening New Testament believers with a "curse" if they don't tithe is neither biblical nor wise. God has already blessed us with every spiritual blessing in Christ, whether we tithe or not. Nevertheless, if we fail to give the Lord "tithes of honor" that are due to Him, we "forfeit" some of the incredible spiritual benefits of the "tithe" but that does not mean that we the "blessed of the Lord" are cursed. However, even a blessed person can hinder or thwart the the flow of the blessings of God in their life, by failing to adhere to certain kingdom principles, of which tithing is one.

When the Lord was giving me the revelation on Tithing under the Order of Melchizedek, He showed me something in Genesis 14:18-19, that I had never seen before. When I saw it, I was pleasantly surprised, but deeply touched. The LORD said to me, "Francis, can you see that Melchizedek first pronounced an un-revokable blessing on Abram's life before He received tithes from Abram. Do you want to know why?" The Lord let His question linger in my mind. Are you kidding me? I wanted to know why and the Lord did not a disappointment. He said, "Francis, under the Order of Melchizedek my people don't tithe to "get blessed" they tithe because they are already blessed. They tithe because they are too blessed not to." I was stunned and excited at the same time. This was a huge contrast with the popular Malachi 3 tithing system where "tithers" are told they will be cursed if they don't tithe and blessed if they do. So under the Malachi 3 tithing system, the blessing of the Lord on the life of the believer is always up for grabs because one incident of failing to tithe can easily erase the condition of "being blessed" on the believer. Its no wonder many people who have been tithing under the dictates of Malachi 3 are never really sure if they are blessed or not. Thankfully under the Order of Melchizedek, every time a "tither" gives "tithes of honor" he or she simply reaffirms the fact that they are already blessed with every spiritual blessing in Christ.

ະຈະຈະຈະຈະຈະ

In my church we never "collect tithes of honor"
from God's people, without taking Holy Communion.

ະຈະຈະຈະຈະຈະ

Tithing to Attest to God's Greatness

Now consider how great this man was, to whom even the patriarch
Abraham gave a tenth of the spoils. Hebrews 7:4

Another reason the Holy Spirit gives us for tithing under the New Testament Melchizedek priesthood of the Lord Jesus Christ is quite profound, to say the least. Using the writer of the book of Hebrews the Holy Spirit gives another consideration as to why and what Abraham tithed for. The scripture declares, "Now consider how great this man was, to whom even the patriarch Abraham gave a tenth of the spoils." This lets us know that first and foremost that Abraham recognized the spiritual loftiness or greatness of Melchizedek and that is why he tithed into His priesthood.

Secondarily, the scriptural text also shows us that "tithing" under the Order of Melchizedek is a prophetic decree to the principalities and powers in the heavenly places that our God is great! So every time children of God give tithes of honor under the Order of Melchizedek they are in essence testifying to His awesome "greatness." Think about this, how can you say "publicly or otherwise" that the LORD is great and He does not show Himself great on your behalf? So why in God's name would any so-called Christian want to rob themselves of an opportunity to testify to God's greatness, if giving tithes carries this powerful testimony? It's no wonder Satan doesn't want God's people to be faithful tithers; he is tortured by the testimony of the tithe in the spirit world.

Tithing Gives Witness to the Resurrection

Here mortal men receive tithes, but there he receives them, of whom it is witnessed that he lives. Hebrews 7:8

In my humble opinion for New Testament believers, there is no motivation for tithing loftier than the one I am about to address here. First, let's break down the expression "Here mortal men receive tithes, but there he receives them." The book of Hebrews was written before the Temple on the Temple mount in Jerusalem was destroyed by the Romans in 70AD, as predicted by the Lord Jesus in the twenty-fourth chapter of Matthew's gospel. This means that even though Jesus had been crucified, resurrected and ascended to heaven the Levites under their corrupt high priest Caiphas continued offering animal sacrifices as usual. The people of Israel continued giving them tithes for their service.

Thankfully, the writer of Hebrews used this scenario to make a clear distinction in the collection of tithes between the two priesthoods (Levi and Melchizedek). The expression "Here (on Earth) mortal men (Levites) receive tithes," is a direct reference to the earthly priesthood of Levi, whereas the second part of the phrase, "but there (in Heaven) he (the resurrected Christ) receives them" is a direct reference to the ongoing and unending priesthood of the Lord Jesus Christ, who has become a priest forever after the Order of Melchizedek. The phrase "receives them" points to an ongoing activity and not a one-time thing!

However, it is the last part of the verse that blew me away. "Of whom it is witnessed that he lives;" The writer of Hebrews is making a profound and earth-shattering statement here. First and foremost the word "witness" used in the text is a judicial terminology. In a courtroom, a "witness" is a person who gives a sworn testimony in front of a judge on the validity of a "thing or event." A credible witness's testimony is usually added to the court's body of evidence for or against the accused. We know from Scripture (Zechariah 3, Luke 18, Job 2, Daniel 7:10, Revelation 12:11) that Satan appears before the Courts of heaven to "accuse" us before God, day and night. However, *every time we give our "tithes," our tithes appear in the Courts of heaven on our behalf to "testify to the resurrection of Jesus."*

Let this truth sink in very deeply! Under the Order of Melchizedek "tithing" is one of the most powerful ways we can attest to the reality of the resurrection of Jesus. When we tithe we are in effect saying to Satan, "move over, you can't have me or my stuff because my Redeemer lives! He is alive and risen from the dead just like He said! Wow, wow, wow! Why in God's good name would children of God want to rob themselves of such a powerful testimony just to keep some extra cash in their pocket? The writer of Hebrews is emphatically saying that if Jesus were not resurrected like Muhammad or Buddha, He wouldn't be able to collect "tithes of His people." So tithing more than any other form of giving in the Bible directly speaks to Christ's resurrection. Hallelujah!

࿂࿂࿂࿂࿂࿂

Every time we give our "tithes," our tithes appear in the Courts of heaven on our behalf to "testify to the resurrection of Jesus."

࿂࿂࿂࿂࿂࿂

Tithing for a Generation Yet Unborn

Even Levi, who receives tithes, paid tithes through Abraham, so to speak, [10] for he was still in the loins of his father when Melchizedek met him. Hebrews 7:9-10

Another equally important reason for tithing is found in the above passage of scripture. The writer of the book of Hebrews declares that Levi who collected tithes from the nation of Israel also "paid tithes" in Abraham because Levi was in the loins of Abram when Melchizedek met him. In other words, God through His foreknowledge could see "Levi" yet unborn in the loins of Abraham. This is when the Holy Spirit dropped a bombshell revelation of one of things God wants us to tithe for.

The writer of Hebrews is unequivocally expressing the idea that Abraham's tithes into Melchizedek secured the future of Levi even though he was till in the loins of his father, Abraham. This means that one of the most powerful things we can tithe for under the Order of Melchizedek is to secure the "future destinies and calling" of our grandchildren yet unborn. I believe some of you reading this book are what you are because of a faithful tithing ancestor. Their tithing secured your destiny and future priesthood.

Tithing as a Sign of a Surrendered Heart

But Abram said to the king of Sodom, "I have raised my hand to the Lord, God Most High, the Possessor of heaven and earth, [23] that I will take nothing, from a thread to a sandal strap, and that I will not take anything that is yours, lest you should say, 'I have made Abram rich'— Genesis 14:22-23

When the LORD was giving me the revelation of tithing under the Order of Melchizedek, He drove my attention to a phrase Abram used when he met with the king of Sodom that relates to the **power of and true foundation of tithing.** When the king of Sodom offered Abram an opportunity to participate in an "unrighteous trade." Abram declares, "I have raised my hand to the Lord, God Most High, the Possessor of heaven and earth." Holy Spirit said to me, *"Francis notice that Abraham compares tithing to the lifting of hands. Francis, what does the lifting of hands mean to you?"* I knew immediately the "lifting of hands" speaks of "surrender." Suddenly, it hit me like a bolt of lighting, "tithing is about surrender, not just giving." Then Holy Spirit placed the icing on the cake. "Francis, under the Order of Melchizedek tithing is an outward manifestation of an inward surrender to God and His kingdom." It became clear to me that trying to exact "tithes" from hearts that are not yet surrendered to God is like pulling teeth.

"Francis, where in the Bible does a man lifting his hands to God lead to a tremendous victory in the marketplace?" The Holy Spirit let the question resonate in my spirit. As an astute bible reader, the story of Moses and the children of Israel quickly came to mind. When the children of Israel were headed to the Promised Land, the Amalekites suddenly impeded their forward advancement. Moses instructed Joshua to go and fight the Amalekites in the Valley while Moses, Aaron, and Hur went up to the mountain. At the top of the Mountain, Moses lifted up his hands to God. Provided he continued to do so the children of Israel prevailed in battle. However, each time he dropped his hands, Joshua and his army began to lose almost immediately. When Aaron and Hur saw this amazing phenomenon, they quickly held up Moses' hands. "So Joshua did what Moses had commanded and fought the army of Amalek. Meanwhile, Moses, Aaron, and Hur climbed to the top of a nearby hill. 11 As long as Moses held up the staff in his hand, the Israelites had the advantage. But whenever he dropped his hand, the Amalekites gained the advantage."

Then the Holy Spirit said to me, "In this scenario who was controlling the fight? Joshua's military skills or Moses' heart of surrender?" It was no brainer! "Lord, its Moses' surrender that was controlling the fight and not the military skills of Joshua." I declared, excitedly. "Francis that is exactly what happens with tithing. When My people give me tithes of honor, I see their hands lifted up, and I immediately begin to fight their marketplace battles. However, if they choose to withhold their tithes, I see them with "hands dropped down" and I let them fight their marketplace battles." I just let the profound implications of the Word of the Lord sink in. Child of God, you have every right to choose not to tithe but get ready to fight your own marketplace battles. Your lack of surrender is indicative that you feel well qualified to handle your own challenges.

❧ఔఄ❧ఔ❧

***Suddenly, it hit me like a bolt of lighting,
"tithing is about surrender, not just giving."***

❧ఔ❧ఔ❧

Tithing to Advance the Kingdom

Then Melchizedek king of Salem brought out bread and wine; he was the priest of God Most High. 19 And he blessed him and said: "Blessed be Abram of God Most High, Possessor of heaven and earth; 20 And blessed be God Most High, Who has delivered your enemies into your hand." And he gave him a tithe of all. Genesis 14:18-20

Seek the Kingdom of God above all else, and live righteously, and he will give you everything you need. Matthew 6:333

Perhaps there is no dispensation of time that is intricately connected to the idea of advancing the kingdom like New Testament living. Dr. Myles Munroe argued that the gospel of the Kingdom is the primary message that Jesus preached. Its no wonder He says in Matthew 6:33, "Seek the Kingdom of God above all else, and live righteously, and he will give you everything you need." This Scripture makes perfect sense when you consider that Jesus is first and foremost a King before He became the atonement for our sins. Since Jesus is a king, it means that He has a kingdom and His kingdom is creation's number one business. This is why New Testament grace living is about passionately advancing the Kingdom of God into every sphere of human enterprise.

Tithing under the Order of Melchizedek is New Testament compliant because its driven by the engines of "grace and faith" for the purpose of advancing the Kingdom. Melchizedek by definition means "king of righteousness;" He was essentially a king over a kingdom of righteousness. Since everything that is given to a king by his subjects becomes part of the royal estate. It's safe to assume that since Abraham gave "tithes" to a king; his tithes were used to advance and support a kingdom. If New Testament grace living is about advancing the Kingdom of God, how can we withhold the giving of tithes without injuring the cause of advancing the Kingdom? Just remember going forward, you are not "tithing for money," but each time you do, you help fuel the advancement of the Kingdom here on Earth.

Tithing to Sanctify Your Avenues for Revenue

Now the king of Sodom said to Abram, "Give me the persons, and take the goods for yourself." 22 But Abram said to the king of Sodom, "I have raised my hand to the Lord, God Most High, the Possessor of heaven and earth, 23 that I will take nothing, from a thread to a sandal strap, and that I will not take anything that is yours, lest you should say, 'I have made Abram rich'— Genesis 14:21-23

The final reason Abraham tithed into Melchizedek priesthood is an interesting but very important one. When Abram took his wife and his household to Egypt during a time of famine, things ended badly for him. In Egypt, in order to preserve his own skin and ensure the survival of his business, Abram leveraged his wife to a demonic system. He allowed Pharaoh to take his wife, Sarah, into his bedchambers. In the meantime, both Abram and Lot were given a lot of "people and financial resources" in exchange for sexual escapades with Sarah. Abram acted and talked as though Sarah was his sister, instead of his wife.

ໆໆໆໆໆໆ

***How can we withhold the giving of tithes
without injuring the cause of advancing the Kingdom?***

ໆໆໆໆໆໆ

Thankfully, God terrorized Pharaoh's palace until he surrendered Sarah back to Abram. Abram left Egypt in the middle of this national scandal and whatever wealth he had accumulated in Egypt under these false pretenses was "tainted at best." Essentially Abram left Egypt with the reproach of Egypt hanging over his head. That stench of being a crook followed him until the day he was intercepted in the Valley of Kings by Melchizedek priesthood. The Holy Spirit said to me, "Francis, Abram's tithes into Melchizedek became the cleansing agent that sanctified the rest of Abram's worldly wealth. After Melchizedek left Abram's wealth was no longer tainted. Tithing under the Order of Melchizedek sanctifies "your avenues for revenue." No matter what you have done in the past may the Lord cause the reproach of Egypt to roll off your shoulders, in Jesus name.

LIFE APPLICATION SECTION

Point to Ponder:

Money is one of the lowest assets in the Kingdom economy because it's the creation of fallen man and not God.

Memory Verse

Therefore if you have not been faithful in the unrighteous mammon, who will commit to your trust the true riches? Luke 16:11

Reflections

1. Why is it spiritually dangerous to be tithing for money?

_____

_____

_____

_____

2. What are true riches?

_____

_____

_____

_____

3. Name one of the most important things to tithe for under the Order of Melchizedek?

_____

_____

_____

_____

Chapter Ten

Where Should I Take My Tithes?

Here mortal men receive tithes, but there he receives them, of whom it is witnessed that he lives. Hebrews 7:8

Whenever I am dealing with the subject of tithing five questions always come up, namely:

- **What is my tithe?**
- **How do I tithe?**
- **Why should I tithe?**
- **Where or who do I give my tithe?**
- **Does every tithe go into the local church?**

These are very important questions concerning the whole subject and process of tithing. It's critical that I answer these questions with supernatural "surgical precision." Perhaps only a few things have come under the "attack of the enemy" more than the giving of "tithes." Please take note of the fact that under the priestly Order of Melchizedek we do not "pay our tithes;" we "give our tithes." This is because there is no amount of money in this earthly economy which can "pay for the sandal straps or shoe laces" of the King of the heavenly Jerusalem, who is also the Priest of God Most High.

Prophet John's Stunning Announcement:

"...Someone is coming soon who is greater than I am—so much greater that I'm not even worthy to stoop down like a slave and untie the straps of his sandals." Mark 1:17

John the Baptist made the above proclamation because he knew that Jesus Christ (Yeshua in Hebrew) who is the King of the heavenly Jerusalem and the High Priest of God Most High, is not of this world. Christ's heavenly Kingdom is "infinitely richer" than anything we can imagine here on earth. His Kingdom also has its own "spiritual currency" which is also "infinitely higher and stronger" than the "combined buying power" of all the best worldly currencies. This is why saying that we are "paying our tithes" when we are dealing with the priesthood of Melchizedek is "an insult and a sure sign of dishonor." How can a "citizen" in any Kingdom pay the "King" when everything he or she owns is already the property of the King? In kingdoms "citizens" do not own anything, they are merely stewards; everything they own belongs to the king. This is why "rediscovering why and how Abraham tithed" is spiritually crucial to our spiritual progress and how we approach the subject of tithing.

Look to Abraham

"Listen to Me, you who follow after righteousness, You who seek the LORD: Look to the rock from which you were hewn, And to the hole of the pit from which you were dug. ² Look to Abraham your father, And to Sarah who bore you; For I called him alone, And blessed him and increased him." Isaiah 51:1-2

The Bible clearly admonishes us to "look to Abraham." This means that even in the area of tithing we must look to Abraham to find "our tithing modality." Henceforth in answering these five questions, we will look to Abraham and his sons after him who continued to walk in the revelation that God had laid out for Abraham.

1. What is my tithe?"

"And blessed be God Most High, who has defeated your enemies for you. Then Abram gave Melchizedek a tenth of all the goods he had recovered." Genesis 14:20

Abraham is the first person to give "tithes" in the progressive revelation of Scripture. When Abraham was returning from the slaughter of the kings, he was intercepted by Melchizedek a priest of God Most High, in the valley of kings (Shaveh). The valley of kings was not too far from the country of Sodom, and it was a popular trading floor, where kings came to trade. This divine encounter with Melchizedek moved Abraham's spirit so deeply that he was compelled by his "deep sense of awe" to give this lofty man a "gift befitting a King." Abraham gave Melchizedek "a tenth or ten percent" of "all the goods which he had recovered from the battlefield." This answers the first question, "What is my tithe?" The tithe is the "tenth or ten percent" of everything we earn in the marketplace or recover from the field of battle.

It's worth noting here that Abraham gave Melchizedek a "tithe of all the goods that he had recovered" from the battlefield, before surrendering the "rest of it" to the king of Sodom. This means that the "tithe" is taken from the "gross" and not from the "net." If you live in the United States, for example, the tithe comes from your "gross salary" before "Uncle Sam" (the US government) takes its share. I personally believe that if many Kingdom citizens would tithe from the "gross and not from the net" as Abraham seemed to have done, we would see more miracles of unexpected tax refunds and favorable tax settlements.

How can a "citizen" in any Kingdom
pay the "King" when everything he or
she owns is already the property of the King?

When we tithe from the gross, I believe that we "sanctify and set apart" that part of our hard earned money that goes to the government in the form of income tax. There are Bible teachers who believe that the "tithe" should really come out of the "net earnings" and not the "gross earnings." The basis of their argument is that the "net earnings" and not the "gross earnings" are a true reflection of what someone really earns. I personally believe in tithing off the gross earnings, but I do not believe that those who tithe from their "net earnings" are necessarily wrong. The most important thing whether you tithe from "gross or net earnings" is that you realize that the "tithe" is the tenth part and that it is consecrated to God.

2. "How do I tithe?"

> *"Consider then how great this Melchizedek was. Even Abraham, the great patriarch of Israel, recognized this by giving him a tenth of what he had taken in battle. Now the law of Moses required that the priests, who are descendants of Levi, must collect a tithe from the rest of the people of Israel, who are also descendants of Abraham. But Melchizedek, who was not a descendant of Levi, collected a tenth from Abraham. And Melchizedek placed a blessing upon Abraham, the one who had already received the promises of God. And without question, the person who has the power to give a blessing is greater than the one who is blessed."* Hebrews 7:4-7 (NLT)

The second question deals with the "prevailing spiritual attitude and mindset" for tithing under the Order of Melchizedek. It's spiritually critical that we find this prevailing attitude and mindset so that we can tithe properly. The Holy Spirit told me, "If My people tithe correctly, money will always follow them as a by-product of tithing for the right reasons." If we do not enshrine ourselves in the same prevailing attitude and mindset as Abraham had, tithing will remain a struggle and a joyless religious activity instead of the catalyst of covenantal blessings that "money cannot buy." Here again, we look to Abraham who was the first "tither."

When Abraham met Melchizedek (the Priest of God Most High), he was deeply moved by this man's lofty "spiritual position as the Priest of God Most High as well as being the King of Salem." The title "King of Salem," we are told in the book of Hebrews, literally means "King of peace" and the name "Melchizedek" means "King of righteousness." In the ancient language of Aramaic, the name "Melchizedek" also means "a King who comes to make everything right by telling the truth."

My dear friend, who else is best, suited to wear these lofty titles other than our Lord Jesus Christ? The immeasurable "power and royal dignity" of this man is what moved Abraham's spirit to give Him a "tithe of all." Abraham gave this man the "tithe of all" out of a "deep sense of awe and heartfelt honor." Abraham gave the tithe to this heavenly man to worship and honor Him. Coincidentally this should be the primary motivation for all "tithers" and not the desire for "more money." Abraham gave Melchizedek the "tithe of all" with the same "mindset" that galvanized nobles and citizens of the Roman Empire when they gave gifts to honor Caesar. This "royal endowment" is not a "salary," because by established "royal protocol" it's well understood that "citizens in a Kingdom" cannot pay the "Crown," but they can give an "endowment of honor." This "royal endowment" is the visible evidence of "the heartfelt honor" that they as kingdom citizens have for the "Crown." When Abraham gave the "tithe of all" to Melchizedek he gave it with this same attitude and mindset. This means that "tithing under the Order of Melchizedek" is the "highest form of tithing" ever revealed by God to mankind.

❧❦❧❦❧❦❧

"Melchizedek" also means "a King who comes
to make everything right by telling the truth."

❧❦❧❦❧❦❧

You Cannot Pay God!

And when Simon saw that through the laying on of the apostles' hands the Holy Spirit was given, he offered them money, [19] saying, "Give me this power also, that anyone on whom I lay hands may receive the Holy Spirit." [20] But Peter said to him, "Your money perish with you because you thought that the gift of God could be purchased with money! Acts 8:18-20

The governing concepts and process of tithing under the priestly Order of Melchizedek are in direct contrast to those of the Levitical (Aaronic) priesthood where "tithing was simply payment for priestly service rendered." Since tithing under the Order of Melchizedek has nothing to do with "paying for priestly services" but rather the "giving of a royal endowment of honor" to the "Crown-King," we cannot use our tithes to manipulate our spiritual leaders to give us the "priestly services" we think we deserve. This mindset may have been acceptable under the Levitical priesthood (Malachi tithing system), but it is both "demonic and dishonoring" when we apply it to Christ's Melchizedek priesthood, which is a Kingdom-centered tithing system.

I am not suggesting that pastors of churches or those who provide spiritual covering should not do their best to offer priestly services to the people in their church or marketplace leaders that they give covering too. However, if our spiritual leaders fall short (no human is perfect), we have "no excuse" as Kingdom citizens to withhold our tithes in our desire to punish our spiritual leaders or the local church. We have no scriptural legal grounds for holding the Kingdom or church of God hostage by withholding our tithes. We cannot be like Simon the sorcerer who felt like the "gift of God" can be purchased with "money."

3. Why should I tithe?

The third question deals with the "prevailing spiritual motivation" for tithing under the Order of Melchizedek. You would be surprised to discover just how many of God's people try to become deceptive the moment they begin to make more money. Suddenly they become astute theologians and ask questions like, "Do I really have to tithe? Why should I tithe when I am under grace? Is not tithing of the Old Testament?" If the truth was told, they are not asking these questions because they are suddenly concerned about these theological issues. The truth of the matter is that they are now asking these tithing questions because they have begun to make more money than they are willing to give to the Lord's work. Their "lust for money" is suddenly challenged by the church's teaching on tithing the more their wealth increases. If the truth was told, they are looking for a way to "stop tithing" without feeling like they are sinning against God. In the United States, they are some members of the gay community who give away over 50% of their income to promote their "gay agenda." Why in Jesus name would people who claim to love Jesus fight like hell to stop giving a meagre 10% of their income?

In answering the question, "Why should I tithe?" We have to look to Abraham. When Abraham tithed, he gave his "tenth of all" as a "royal endowment of honor" to Melchizedek who was a Priest of God Most High and King of righteousness and peace. The late Dr. Myles Munroe in his book Kingdom Principles says that "democratic societies" were born out of "rebellion" to Kingdom principles of governance. Men were tired of living under the authority of abusive and sometimes corrupt "Monarchs," and so they decided to find new forms of government. Whereas we can surely empathize with the fathers of the American democratic society, who were running away from an abusive monarch in England, one cannot help but wonder how much of the Kingdom reality we lost when we built democratic nations that are not based on a Kingdom model."

The truth of the matter is that in a kingdom the "king owns everything that is in his kingdom, including the people." This first statement by itself should abolish all struggles about tithing because in God's Kingdom everything we own already belongs to the Lord. Giving the Lord the "tithe" that He has specially "consecrated" for the advancement of His Kingdom should be the least of our struggles. Interesting enough American Christians are some of the most zealous and faithful tax payers in the United States. The average income tax that most Americans pay is usually between 20 to 30% of one's annual income.

So why is tithing, (*giving 10% of earned income to the Lord's work*) such a controversial subject within the Body of Christ? I believe it is because there is a very powerful spiritual blessing attached to the tithe that every demon in hell is terrified of. In a kingdom, citizens do not "own anything; everyone is simply a steward" of the king's property. Under the Order of Melchizedek "tithes" are not "payment for services rendered," they are a "royal endowment of honor" from Kingdom citizens for the "continued privilege" of living and working in the King's domain (Earth).

❧❧❧❧❧❧❧

God's children have no scriptural grounds
for holding the Kingdom or church of

God hostage by withholding our tithes.
જ્જ્જ્જ્જ્જ

The previous statement answers our question, "Why should I tithe?" We should tithe because "everything we own" including the air we breathe and the inherent talents we possess, belongs to our King of righteousness and peace, who is also the High Priest of the eternal priesthood of all believers. This would explain why God could legally and righteously give the land of Palestine to the Jewish nation who came out of Egypt without consulting the "inhabitants of the land of Canaan." God is the King of the universe, possessor of heaven and earth. He can give His "Crown land" or earthly riches to whomsoever He chooses. This means that we should tithe for as long as we "call ourselves citizens of the Kingdom of God here on earth."

Kingdom citizens must always give Jesus Christ his "befitting royal endowment" of tithe. It is my personal conviction that continued failure to "honor God with our tithes" may eventually result in the King of kings "removing His seal of approval" from our lives. King Jesus may also "remove us from our position of stewardship in His Kingdom." This is not to say that the lack of tithing can result in someone losing their salvation. Our salvation is based solely upon the finished work of Christ on the cross and not on our human efforts. However, we must not confuse our "salvation" with our "position of stewardship" in God's Kingdom. Stewardship is always based upon our faithfulness to God and the principles that govern His Kingdom.

> Let a man so account of us, as of the ministers of Christ, and stewards of the mysteries of God. Moreover it is required in stewards, that a man be found faithful. 1 Corinthians 4:1-2 (KJV)

Under the Levitical priesthood, non-tithers were chastised with a curse, which "allowed" the devourer to devour their finances or their agricultural products (Malachi 3:10-12). However, under the Order of Melchizedek non-tithers are not "cursed," but they risk losing the "King's seal of approval" upon their position of stewardship in the Kingdom. Under Christ's Melchizedek priesthood if we do not tithe,

God will not place us under a "financial curse" because He has already blessed us with every spiritual blessing in heavenly places (Ephesians 1:3). However, our failure to tithe will slowly but surely begin to "mortgage or undermine" our access to "things money cannot buy."

❧❧❧❧❧❧❧
Kingdom citizens must always give Jesus Christ his "befitting royal endowment" of tithe.
❧❧❧❧❧❧❧

4. Where or who do I give my tithe?

This question deals with the "prevailing spiritual flow' that "tithes" take under the priestly Order of Melchizedek or what I call the "Genesis 14:18-20" pattern of tithing. Under the priestly Order of Melchizedek, the spiritual flow of the giving of the tithe is a "two stream" approach. This two-stream approach answers the question of where and to whom you give your tithe. Before diving into this very critical question, I must first acknowledge the wide diversity in how churches around the world view this critical topic. It is not my desire to divide the Body of Christ over this matter but rather to share my core convictions and the reasons behind them. I do this with utmost humility. However, I will not be offended if you disagree with me.

I only humbly request that if you do disagree with me that you would do so not out of your preconceived conclusions on this subject without giving my arguments the scriptural introspection that they deserve. I have observed that too many times "Tithing" is either defended or opposed from an emotional point of view or by preconceived ideas than by spiritual precedence and biblical facts.

Please do not throw the baby out with the bathwater.

I also want to caution senior pastors within the global church to refrain from setting up legalistic top-down "tithing" structures so as not to force any believer to do anything contrary to their free will or conscience. The New Testament never gives spiritual leaders the authority to force Kingdom citizens to violate their conscience. Tithing is very important, but it must not be done by compulsion, for the Lord loves a cheerful giver.

1. *The first stream of tithing is the giving of "tithes" to the "local church," where you are a member.*
2. *The second stream of tithing is the giving of "tithes" to a "Man of God or Spiritual Covering," the Lord has set over your life.*

The First Stream of Tithing

The first stream of tithing addresses the question of "how church members or spiritual sons and daughters in the house (local church) ought to tithe." I cannot tell you just how many times well-meaning Christians have walked up to me and said to me, "Brother Myles, God told me to give my tithe to an orphanage or the Red Cross." I certainly appreciate their philanthropic generosity, but their gift cannot be called "tithes," even though the amount given equals 10% of their income. Needless to say, the tithe almost always goes to your local church if you belong to one. This is because God has already placed you under the "spiritual covering" of the "greater one" (your senior pastor), who is anointed by God to "feed you, with heavenly bread and wine."

When Jacob was fleeing from Esau he came to a place called "Bethel," which literally means "the assembled house of God." He spent the night there and slept on one of the stones of that place. While he was sleeping, he had a life-changing encounter with God in a dream. In this dream, Jacob saw an open heaven and a ladder, which stretched from the earth to the third heaven. Angels were ascending and descending on this ladder.

The House of God: Gateway to Heaven

"Then Jacob awoke from his sleep and said,—Surely the LORD is in this place, and I wasn't even aware of it! But he was also afraid and said,—What an awesome place this is! It is none other than the house of God, the very gateway to heaven! The next morning Jacob got up very early. He took the stone he had rested his head against, and he set it upright as a memorial pillar. Then he poured olive oil over it. He named that place Bethel (which means—house of God), although the name of the nearby village was Luz. Then Jacob made

this vow: —If God will indeed be with me and protect me on this journey, and if he will provide me with food and clothing, and if I return safely to my father's home, then the LORD will certainly be my God. And this memorial pillar I have set up will become a place for worshiping God, and I will present to God a tenth of everything he gives me." Genesis 28:16-22

When Jacob woke up the following morning, he was deeply moved by what he had seen and heard in his dream. He realized that the place where he was standing was none other than the "house of God." The "house of God" is a prophetic picture of the local church. The local church is the local expression of Christ in a particular geographical location. Once Jacob realized that the place on which he was standing was the "house of God" and the "Gate of heaven," he made a "covenant of tithe" with the God of this place. At this particular time in Jacob's life, Jacob had not yet become a "father of his own house." He was still part of "his father's house." This is a very important observation because Jacob's "covenant of tithe" with the "house of God" is the same covenant God expects all church members to make with Him.

ക്കൈൟ

Tithing is very important, but it must not be done by compulsion, for the Lord loves a cheerful giver.

ക്കൈൟ

This means that "if you are not the senior pastor/minister of your own church," your "tithes" (in most cases) belongs to the house local church you attend regularly. This also means that giving your tithe to a "missionary you simply feel sorry for or the Red Cross" is tantamount to "breaking faith" with God and the local church that you attend." This kind of inaccurate patterns of tithing will fail to draw the covenantal blessings of God upon your life. Tithing under the Order of Melchizedek, even under the Levitical priesthood always moves in the direction of a "priesthood" the Lord has chosen to cover you spiritually.

The Second Stream of Tithing

Now consider how great this man was, to whom even the patriarch Abraham gave a tenth of the spoils. Hebrews 7:4

The second stream of tithing addresses the question of how "some marketplace leaders, itinerant ministers or senior pastors" of a church ought to tithe. This stream of tithing is "dual directional." In this second stream of tithing the tithe is "tithed up and across!" When it is "tithed up" the tithe goes to a man or woman of God, whom the senior pastor, itinerant minister or marketplace leader regards as the primary God-ordained spiritual father or covering. This is a person from whom the senior pastor, itinerant minister or marketplace leader receives his or her primary apostolic input. Like Melchizedek brought "bread and wine" (Genesis 14:18) to Abram, this "person" provides spiritual nourishment and accountability for the continued spiritual development of the senior pastor, itinerant minister or marketplace leader.

When the tithe is "tithed across," it goes to a "God-ordained group of peer-level senior ministers" whom the senior pastor, itinerant minister or marketplace leader has chosen to be spiritually accountable to. This group of God-ordained peer level senior ministers will then represent the "Order of Melchizedek" to the senior pastor, itinerant minister or marketplace leader. Unfortunately, the lack of functional spiritual accountability to a "spiritual covering" by many senior pastors, itinerant ministers or marketplace leaders has brought great damage to the cause of Christ and tarnished the image of the church in general. The Church's public image got tarnished when some of these senior pastors, itinerant ministers or marketplace leaders fell into sexual sin, spousal abuse or were caught stealing money from their churches, ministries or businesses.

This is why rediscovering the power of the priestly Order of Melchizedek is so important to the global Church. Only the priestly Order of Melchizedek can effectively "heal the lack of functional spiritual accountability" which exists among so many senior pastors, itinerant ministers, and marketplace leaders.

Tithing Upwards!

"But Melchizedek, who was not a descendant of Levi, collected a tenth from Abraham. And Melchizedek placed a blessing upon Abraham, the one who had already received the promises of God. ⁷ And without question, the person who has the power to give a blessing is greater than the one who is blessed." Hebrews 7:6-7

From my observation, I believe the greatest culprits of "inaccurate tithing patterns" are apostolic leaders or senior pastors of churches. I know this firsthand because as the senior pastor of a thriving church, I was also guilty of "cheating" on my tithing patterns. What am I referring to? I am referring to the practice of senior pastors "tithing" into their congregation. I really believe that this practice is inherently flawed. I really believe that every senior pastor or minister needs a pastor/spiritual father or a group of peer-level ministers whom he or she can submit his or her life to.

I am convinced that as flesh and blood humans we are all, a scandal waiting to happen when left to our devices. This peer-level accountability group can never be a group of "Yes men or women," who lack the power to bring down the rod of correction in our lives. What we call our spiritual covering must be able to bring us under the knife of God's correction, or we are wasting our tithes tithing into a spiritual covering that simply rubber-stamps our spiritual arrogance and deceptive tendencies.

Our spiritual covering must have "teeth to it." If our spouses cannot call our so-called "spiritual covering" and get help when we are misrepresenting God in our home, then our so-called spiritual covering is NOT operating under the Order of Melchizedek. Melchizedek, the eternal King-Priest, did not intercept Abram to rubber stamp Abram's deceptive behavior in the Marketplace. On the contrary, He came to circumcise him with the sword of God's Word, and He never apologized for it. When Melchizedek left, Abram was a changed man. This life-transforming spiritual covering is "worth" tithing into.

This "pastor/spiritual father or accountability group" will then represent "the Order of Melchizedek" to the senior pastor/minister who has submitted his or her life to the same. I highly recommend that senior pastors/ministers "give all or a reasonable portion" of their personal tithe to the "pastor/spiritual father or accountability group" who are laboring to keep them in the straight and narrow path. The remaining portion of their personal tithe can then be sown in their local church if they are not comfortable giving it all to their spiritual covering. However, I believe the "more excellent way" is for senior pastors/ministers to sow "their entire personal tithe" into the life and ministry of their spiritual father/covering or into the ministries of their "peer-level accountability group."

I really believe that every senior pastor or minister needs a pastor/spiritual father or a group of peer-level ministers whom he or she can submit his or her life to.

The Builder has More Honor than the House!

"For this man (Jesus) was counted worthy of more glory than Moses, inasmuch as he who hath builded the house hath more honour than the house. ⁴For every house is builded by some man; but he that built all things is God." Hebrews 3:3-4 (KJV, adapted by author)

The above passages of Scripture are the reason I believe that the practice of senior pastors/ministers tithing into their own local church or itinerant ministry is an "inaccurate pattern of tithing." The apostle Paul compares the great prophet Moses to our Lord Jesus Christ and comes to the staggering conclusion that our Lord Jesus Christ was and is immeasurably more glorious than Moses. I am sure that everyone reading this book would agree with Paul's summation. However, the apostle Paul goes a step further in his desire to prove and quench any doubts as to the superiority of Christ over the great prophet, Moses. Please remember that the book of Hebrews was an apologetic book written to convince Jewish believers that they were making the right choice in choosing Jesus Christ over Moses.

Paul goes on to say that the "difference in glory and honor" between Jesus Christ and Moses, is similar to the one that exists between the "builder of the house" and the "house itself." This verse shows us one of the "most neglected apostolic principles" that God uses in building His Kingdom here on earth. When God is building His Kingdom, He places "more glory and honor" on the "builder of the house" (the senior pastor/ set man) than on the "house" (congregation) itself. When people drive through a very expensive neighborhood to look at expensive and breath taking, multimillion-dollar homes, they know intuitively that the person who built the gorgeous and expensive home has more splendor than the house itself. This is why people often inquire as to who owns and lives in a beautiful house that they deeply admire.

Denominations that do not esteem senior pastors over their churches while placing undue emphasis on the congregation are guilty of violating one of the most "important principles for Kingdom building." Overzealous elders or deacons who place "more honor" on the congregation than they have placed on their senior pastor sadden me deeply. They forget the fact that their senior pastor is the man or woman that God is using to build the local congregation. The apostle Paul goes on further and points to the "marked difference in glory and honor" between Melchizedek and Abraham.

In so doing the apostle Paul underscores another very important "apostolic principle" God uses in building His Kingdom here on earth. Paul argues that since Melchizedek is the one who blessed Abraham, he was "greater in stature" than Abraham. Paul then identifies the spiritual principle behind his conclusion. In the "spiritual realm" the "lesser or subordinate" is "blessed by the greater or senior minister." This spiritual principle is even more so true for those of us who live under Christ's Melchizedek priesthood. This "apostolic Kingdom-building principle" of the "lesser being blessed by the greater" is especially true when one is considering how the tithe is disbursed.

When Paul was teaching on this principle of the "lesser being blessed by the greater," he was employing this principle in the context of Abraham's encounter with Melchizedek. Paul was using this principle to explain what happened to Abraham when he tithed into Melchizedek. The "lesser one (Abraham) received from the greater one (Melchizedek) the power to actualize the promises that God gave him." The spiritual implication is staggering but obvious. The spiritual implication is simply this: the "tithe" always travels in the "direction of the greater" and never flows from the "greater" to the "lesser." The "greater" can either be one individual or a group of peer-level leaders whom the senior pastor/minister submits his or her life to.

❧❧❧❧❧❧

Overzealous elders or deacons who place "more honor" on the congregation than they have placed on their senior pastor sadden me deeply.

❧❧❧❧❧❧

Questions Demanding Answers

And without question, the person who has the power to give a blessing is greater than the one who is blessed." Hebrews 7:7

Here are two million-dollar questions that every senior pastor or minister must answer honestly. *"If the builder of the house has more glory and honor than the house and the lesser is blessed by, the greater, how can pastors justify tithing into their own church?"* How can you as the senior pastor/minister "tithe down, instead of tithing up or across" and still expect the "covenantal blessing of tithing" to flow into your life? When we as senior pastors tithe into the congregation that we are leading, one way or the other, we still end up controlling how our "tithes" are spent because we have oversight over the money that comes into our church. We can easily find a way to make our "tithes" benefit us personally. I truly believe that when many senior pastors/ministers are delivered from these "inaccurate patterns of tithing," there will be an "explosion of tithing" in the global church. I rest my case.

These inaccurate patterns of tithing among senior pastors/ministers would also explain why God has not given us the grace to lead everyone in our churches into a lifestyle of complete obedience to God in the area of tithing. How can God give us this power when we are actively cheating on our personal tithe? As senior pastors/ministers giving our entire personal tithe to our own churches is like "taking money from one of our pockets and then putting it into the other pocket." This is what many senior pastors call tithing. The problem behind this practice is simply this: "One way or the other the tithe money we give to our own church always ends up under our control!" How would we feel if our people also began to tithe into themselves? Selah. According to 2 Corinthians 10:6, we can only punish all disobedience when our own obedience to the Lord is fulfilled!

5. Does every tithe go to my local church?

> *"Then Melchizedek king of Salem also brought out bread and wine, he was the priest of God most high and He blessed him and said, Blessed be Abram of God most high, possessor of heaven and earth who has delivered your enemies into your hand and he gave him a tithe of all."* Genesis 14:18-20 (KJV)

This final question – "Does every tithe go into my local church?" This is a very intricate question that must be handled with surgical precision and forensic aptitude. Several years back had I been asked the same question, my answer would have been "Yes, every tithe always goes into the local church." Like most pastors, I would have defended my answer to this final question with my life. But God has since proved me wrong both by revelation and by personal experience.

The Holy Spirit showed me that there are special cases in which the tithe does not go to the local church of the person attending the same. However, even though these special cases do not violate the principles of tithing under the Order of Melchizedek, they are the EXCEPTION and not the rule. These special cases affect and apply to only a small section of the body of Christ. The tithes of the majority of the body of Christ generally belong to the local church that they attend on a regular basis. This is because the local church is the primary embassy that God has appointed to advance the Kingdom in the community or City that the church (local congregation) is based in.

Before I explain these special cases of tithing, I need to lay a foundation for what I'm about to say. Tithing under the Order of Melchizedek is always predicated on who is the primary channel that God is using to feed us the heavenly bread and wine that is helping us to enter into our prophetic destiny in God. This principle establishes who has the right to the tithe in our life. This primary channel has to be a constant prophetic voice into our lives and not just a "one night stand" prophetic or apostolic voice so to speak. In most cases, the person who has the right to the tithes is usually the senior pastor of the local church that we attend on a regular basis, since he or she is the primary source of the bread of deliverance and the wine of revelation for the local church (congregation). Just to be clear, I am NOT suggesting that all the tithes of the members of a local congregation be given to the senior pastor personally, but to the local church that he or she pastors.

Over the years, God has introduced me to members of that small section of the body of Christ, who did not feel comfortable tithing into the local church that they were attending, because they felt that the pastor of the church that they were attending was not the primary channel of the heavenly bread and the wine (spiritual nourishment) that they were living on in their march towards their God-given destiny. They had no problem giving their offerings to their new pastor; they just struggled with giving their tithes to a pastor who did not represent the Order of Melchizedek to them.

 festoon ornament

***When senior pastors tithe into their congregation
that they are leading, one way or the other,
they end up controlling how their "tithes" are used.***

festoon ornament

At first, I thought this was arrogance and spiritual immaturity on the part of this special class of Kingdom citizens who found themselves in this type of situation in churches across the world. For a while, I dismissed this special class of Kingdom citizens as a bunch of arrogant and rebellious saints. Thankfully, God pulled the carpet from under me when He put me in a situation where I became part of that small section of the body of Christ, that did not feel comfortable giving tithes into the local church that I was attending at the time. This small section of the body of Christ usually includes many itinerant ministers and some marketplace leaders.

In 2001, I moved to Oklahoma City. I started attending a church that I had helped to grow while I was still living in Chicago. The pastor of the church was a dear friend of mine, but he was definitely not my spiritual father or covering even though attending his church while I lived in the city was the most logical choice for me. It was both fun and convenient. I sowed a lot of offerings into my friend's church, but I continued to give my tithe to my spiritual father, who was the primary channel of the heavenly bread and wine that I needed to move forward into my destiny. To my friend's credit, he respected my desire to remain honorable in my relationship to the man that God had raised to represent the Order of Melchizedek in my life.

Many Instructors, Few Fathers!

For though you might have ten thousand instructors in Christ, yet you do not have many fathers; for in Christ Jesus I have begotten you through the gospel. 1 Corinthians 4:15

While I was attending my friend's church, I served as a spiritual advisor to his board of elders, but I never became an elder in his church. This is because it would have been out of order for me to be an elder in a church that I did not feel comfortable tithing into. No one should ever be an elder in a church that they do not feel comfortable tithing into. However, I was very generous in the offerings that I gave into my friend's church. But like I said at the beginning of this section, this special class of Kingdom citizens is the EXCEPTION and not the rule. I know that there some pastors of churches who will be very annoyed or irritated with me for mentioning such an exception.

However, reality is simply this; it is better for people to tithe by revelation than by compulsion. Revelation always wins over compulsion. If scaring the saints with the curse of Malachi 3 had been very successful in improving the levels of tithing in the global church, the Holy Spirit would never have summoned me to write a book like the one that you are reading! Furthermore, globally "tithes" have been in sharp decline under the Malachi 3 tithing system, because the Holy Spirit is shutting down this inaccurate tithing system.

Let me simulate a real-life scenario that often happens to help cement the fact that there are special cases where the tithe does not necessarily go into the local church of the person giving the tithe. While John Doe was living in Florida, Pastor Jesse became John Doe's pastor and spiritual father. Pastor Jesse really worked very hard on discipling John Doe and turning his business around. While living in Florida, John Doe attended Pastor Jesse's church and never missed a service. John Doe was so grateful to God that he had a caring and loving spiritual father like Pastor Jesse.

Unfortunately, John Doe's business moved him to New York, where he began to attend New York Fellowship Church (fictional name) pastored by Jim Ducker. Even though John Doe enjoys his new church in New York, his highest loyalty is still attached to Pastor Jesse, whom he regards as his spiritual father. John Doe's deep sense of loyalty and honor compels him to send his tithes to Pastor Jesse's church even though he now regularly attends Pastor Jim Ducker's church. Those who are very dogmatic about the fact that the tithe always goes into the local church that a person attends would judge John Doe's actions very harshly and call him rebellious. But how can John Doe deny the fact that the primary source of the heavenly bread and wine that is changing his life is coming from his relationship with Pastor Jesse, his spiritual father, even though he now lives in New York where he attends Pastor Jim Ducker's church.

Under the Order of Melchizedek, John Doe's tithing pattern is completely acceptable, provided that Pastor Jesse and John Doe maintain a healthy and ongoing vibrant spiritual father-son relationship. But like I said at the beginning, this scenario is the EXCEPTION and not the rule. For the most part (about 95% of the time) the tithe of God's people belongs to the local church that they attend. As a general disclaimer, this section is not meant or intended to give license to anyone to tithe wherever they feel like it; only those who are spiritually immature and unstable may come up with such an erroneous conclusion.

My Sheep Hear My Voice

My sheep hear my voice, and I know them, and they follow me.
John 10:27

Pastors who are afraid that this section on the special cases of tithing might cause their people to give their tithes to their favorite Televangelist, author or teacher need to heed Christ's admonition in John 10:27. Jesus Christ, the great shepherd of the sheep gave us three key qualities of a true shepherd or pastor. These three qualities represent the "honor" that God has placed upon every true shepherd who truly loves and cares for the sheep.

(i.) *Jesus said the Sheep always listen to the voice of the shepherd.*

(ii.) *The true shepherd has a very real and meaningful relationship with the sheep, and know his sheep intimately.*

(iii.) *Sheep will naturally follow the voice and leadership of the Shepherd.*

The point I am driving at is this: any true shepherd or pastor never has to worry about his or her sheep following the voice of a stranger. Consequently, "true sheep" will not give tithes that belong to the house of the Shepherd to another. Senior pastors (of whom I am one) need to learn to trust the Holy Spirit, who is the one Jesus Christ commissioned to assign His sheep (His people) to the shepherd or pastor of His choice. Gone should be the days when pastors fight over church members. Fighting over church members is another form of idolatry because it exalts human power over God's power. The apostle Paul made it very clear that it is God who gives the increase, not our intimidation or manipulation.

This book is NOT written to steer people away from tithing to their local church, by no means. I am a pastor over a local church in Phoenix, Arizona and I would never write a book that would undermine the critical importance of tithing into the local church. Rather, this book is meant to resuscitate the dying engines of tithing in the Body of Christ by restoring all proper, biblical channels of tithing, including channels that religious tradition may consider controversial. Far from being controversial, I am only trying to be very practical and realistic. When Kingdom citizens realize that they are NOT being coerced into tithing, but are simply being reintroduced to a more excellent way of tithing, the numbers of committed tithers within the Body of Christ will rise exponentially.

ঙ৯৯৯৯৯৯

Any true shepherd or pastor never has to worry
about his or her sheep following the voice of a stranger.

ঙ৯৯৯৯৯৯

Here is a Second Scenario

I have met several dear children of God who have given up on the organized church for a season because they were hurt deeply by the church or its leadership. Many of these people have told me that they would rather watch Christian television on Sunday morning than drive to any church. While I disagree with their choice, I do empathize with their emotional and spiritual disillusionment with many of the flaws of the institutional church and with certain leaders who scandalized themselves. *God wants His people to learn how to live and function effectively with the rest of the Body of Christ, and the local church is the best place for this important spiritual exercise.* However, my acknowledgment of the dilemma that many of these Kingdom citizens find themselves in does not solve their tithing dilemma. Since they are not part of an established local church, how do they get to participate in the Kingdom principle of tithing?

My answer to these believers, while they are in this season, is that they need to send their tithes to a Televangelist, author or preacher of the gospel whom they feel supernaturally drawn to, who is also feeding their spirit with that precious heavenly bread and wine. It is better for Kingdom citizens to be tithing into a ministry that propagates the gospel of the Kingdom than to throw away their "tithes" into secular charitable organizations like the Red Cross (I know of disfranchised believers who are doing this). By sending their tithes to the Televangelist, author or preacher that they have identified as the primary channel of that precious heavenly bread and wine, they can still participate in the covenant blessings of the tithe, while they are waiting on God to heal them from the "hurts and offenses" that they picked up in the organized church.

However, I strongly caution these Christians not to allow themselves to dwell in the valley of indecision for too long. God created us for the community. God wants us to be part of a community of shared values and interests. Being part of a stable and caring local church is God's best and preferred method for planting us in a Kingdom community with people of like precious faith. *The local church expression is also the best place for God to groom us into the image of His dear Son Jesus.*

Here is a Third Scenario

So continuing daily with one accord in the temple, and breaking bread from house to house, they ate their food with gladness and simplicity of heart. Acts 2:46

There are a growing number of online and house churches that are mushrooming all over the world. This online or house church movement is not a phenomenon that the organized church can simply ignore or wish away. The truth of the matter is that there are thousands of born-again believers who belong to an online or house church. Many of them have no desire to join the ranks of the organized church. Since most houses churches have no paid staff or full-time ministers, *how do members of these house fellowships disburse their tithes of honor?*

Once again, every member of the Body of Christ is under Christ's Melchizedek priesthood whether he or she knows it or not. Under the Order of Melchizedek, the Holy Spirit always raises a man or a group of persons who are ordained and sanctified to represent this eternal priestly Order in the life of the believer. This person or persons must be the primary channel of the precious "heavenly bread and wine" (spiritual nourishment) that God will be using to sustain us in our forward advancement towards our God-given destiny. Once a believer who attends a house church fellowship identifies such a person or persons, *they need to start tithing into this person or accountability group to activate the covenantal blessings of the tithe.* There is no New Testament believer who is excused from participating in the kingdom principle of tithing. Under the New Testament, "tithes" are used to fuel and finance the advancement of the Kingdom of God. So what follower of Christ is excluded from financing this sacred task?

֍֍֍֍֍֍֍

The local church expression is also
the best place for God to groom us into
the image of His dear Son Jesus.

֍֍֍֍֍֍֍

While many of those who attend house churches are very genuine in their motivation, there is also a growing number of spiritual dissidents who join house church fellowships simply to avoid the giving of "tithes" and being spiritually accountable. To this group of Christians, I can only say that any person who is determined to avoid the giving of tithes will NEVER know the incredible privilege of living under Christ's Melchizedek priesthood. This is because, without Abraham's encounter with Melchizedek's priesthood (Genesis 14), the whole practice of tithing would have been nonexistent. It is the eternal Order of Melchizedek that introduced humanity (Abram) to the spiritual technology of "tithing" in order to advance the Kingdom of God, as well as fuel the fulfillment of our God-given destiny here on earth. I am just glad that God has never gone out of His way to avoid giving us all the incredible benefits of salvation like some of His people do in their endeavor to avoid the giving of tithes to His Kingdom. *Only the judgment seat of Christ will reveal the far-reaching spiritual ramifications of their gross error and greed.*

LIFE APPLICATION SECTION

Point to Ponder:

The man (senior pastor) who builds the house (local church) has more honor than the house they have built. But the builder of all things is God.

Memory Verse:

"Listen to Me, you who follow after righteousness, You who seek the LORD: Look to the rock from which you were hewn, And to the hole of the pit from which you were dug. 2 Look to Abraham your father, And to Sarah who bore you; For I called him alone, And blessed him and increased him." Isaiah 51:1-2

Questions to Consider:

1. What is the tithe?

_____

_____

_____

_____

2. Why should I tithe?

_____

_____

_____

_____

3. Where do I give my tithe?"

_____

_____

_____

_____

Chapter Eleven

Finding the Lost Coin

"Or what woman, having ten silver coins, if she loses one coin, does not light a lamp, sweep the house, and search carefully until she finds it? ⁹ And when she has found it, she calls her friends and neighbors together, saying, 'Rejoice with me, for I have found the piece which I lost!' ¹⁰ Likewise, I say to you, there is joy in the presence of the angels of God over one sinner who repents." Luke 15:8-10

Whenever the Lord Jesus wanted to unravel deep and hidden mysteries of the kingdom He would resort to parables. The master storyteller used these parables to unpack deep kingdom truths and principles that otherwise would be difficult to grasp. In the parable of the "Lost coin" Jesus tells much about how to restore the important kingdom principle of tithing. We will examine the above passage of Scripture for these precious nuggets of truth. We will first start by unpacking several prophetic elements contained in the parable.

Decoding the Prophetic Elements

1.) *The "Woman" in the story represents the local church*
2.) *The "Ten coins" represents God's 100% blessing that comes from being under divine order*
3.) *The Lost coin was the "tenth coin," which represents the tithe*

4.) *The Lamp represents "revelation or divine illumination."*
5.) *Sweeping the house represents "mental transformation through revelatory teaching."*
6.) *Friends in the story represent members of a local church*
7.) *Neighbors represent people outside their church who are impacted by the outreach ministry of the local church*

Decrypting the Parable

The parable of the lost coin tells us that there was a woman (local church) who had ten coins. Since ten is the number of divine order, it means that she was walking in divine order. When we walk in divine order, we guarantee God's full or 100% percent blessing on our life. However, Satan always tries to derail people or organizations that are walking in divine order. In the course of time, something went out of order in the woman's life as captured by the phrase, if she loses one coin. She somehow lost the "tenth" coin. The tenth coin represents the Lord's tithe. "Consider then how great this Melchizedek was. Even Abraham, the great patriarch of Israel, recognized this by giving him a tenth of what he had taken in battle Hebrews 7:4." In the parable of the lost coin Jesus wanted us to know that there is nothing the devil fights in the most in the life of a church like the "tithe or tenth coin." In Nigeria and many other countries the giving or "paying of tithes" as proponents of Malachi 3 tithing system call it; has come under tremendous spiritual attack. The devil truly hates the "power and testimony" of the "tenth coin."

۶۹۶۹۶۹۶۹
<center>The lost tenth coin represents the Lord's tithe.</center>
۶۹۶۹۶۹۶۹

Jesus continues the parable by saying the woman went on a frantic and determined search to find the lost coin. The following phrase captures this frantic search, does not light a lamp, sweep the house, and search carefully until she finds it? My ministry as a prophet to the nations has taken me to many countries, and I have not been in a country where the church is not frantically searching for the "lost tenth coin." They can't understand why besides their best efforts the "tithing" in the church is in decline. Fewer and fewer people are tithing. Thankfully, Jesus' parable besides being diagnostic is also a harbinger of things to come. The parable shows that there is coming a global worldwide revival of tithing in the body of Christ, which will result in millions of souls being swept into the Kingdom. Hallelujah! In the parable, Jesus does tell us that the "Woman (the church)" found the lost "tenth coin" and great was her rejoicing. I believe that God will use books such as the one you are reading as catalysts for this "end-time revival in tithing." In the parable, Jesus gives us 4 master keys for "recovering the lost tenth coin." We will discuss these keys in great detail.

#1: Light a Lamp

"Or what woman, having ten silver coins, if she loses one coin, does not light a lamp, sweep the house, and search carefully until she finds it? Luke 15:8

According to Jesus the first master key for recovering the "lost tenth coin" is "lighting a lamp." What does this expression mean? Lighting of a lamp represents allowing Holy Spirit inspired revelation to flood the minds of the people in your church. The Bible is very clear that revelation can actually reach the most difficult of people. Revelation allows to see "things or subjects" from God's vantage point. The Psalmist boldly declares, *"The entrance of Your Word gives light; it gives understanding to the simple."* This passage from Psalm 119:130 lets us know that when the Word of God enters our heart, it brings supernatural illumination in matters of the heart that we could not have conceived by natural means. The Word of God also brings an understanding of kingdom principles to our mental faculties. This means that a spiritual concept that was previously difficult for us to grapple with suddenly becomes palatable to mind.

꧁꧂꧁꧂꧁꧂
Revelation allows to see "things or subjects" from God's vantage point.
꧁꧂꧁꧂꧁꧂

Restoring the lost tenth coin requires that we engage a higher revelation than the one that caused us to lose the "tenth coin" in the first place. Here is a wisdom key # "A problem can never be solved at the same level of thinking it was created at!" I am convinced that the main reason the global church has its grip on "tithing" is due to its excessive use of the outdated Malachi 3 tithing system. If the body of Christ continues to exact the tithe using Malachi 3, the declining levels of tithing in the church will only get worse. This book offers the church and every believer "higher revelation on tithing and loftier reasons for tithing" than the ones purported by the Malachi 3 tithing system.

#2: Sweep the House

"Or what woman, having ten silver coins, if she loses one coin, does not light a lamp, sweep the house, and search carefully until she finds it? Luke 15:8

The most fascinating part of the parable of the lost coin is that Jesus implies that the "lost tenth coin" was lost within the "Woman's (local church) house." This is quite interesting. This goes to show you that when "tithing' begins to go drop in any church, its usually because many of the people attending the church, come to service with their tithes in their pockets and then leave with "tithes" that they should have left with the church they attend regularly. Consequently, the tithe (tenth coin) is never lost in the marketplace; it is always lost among the body of believers. It is not that your church members suddenly don't have the money. It's usually because something has happened in their heart, which has becoming a stumbling block to tithing like they used to.

One of the key solutions to this problem according to Jesus is "sweeping the house." Sweeping the house implies saturating the minds of God's children in your church with "good and balanced teaching on money, stewardship, and tithing." Sweeping the house is allowing the Holy Spirit to uproot all the false teachings in your mind that the devil is using to challenger the knowledge of Christ in your life. I have discovered that many sincere children of God really want to tithe, but "false teaching" like "If you don't pay your tithes you are going to hell;" has "put off" former and future potential tithes. The false doctrine or teaching that money is the best God can give His children for tithing must be "swept" out of the minds of future church members. It never ceases to amazes just how many Christians start tithing after hearing me teach on "Tithing under the Order of Melchizedek." This is the surprising part for many pastors. However, it proves that some people are not tithing because they don't know any better and those who do, don't believe that Malachi 3 tithing system applies to New Testament believers.

#3: Search Carefully

"Or what woman, having ten silver coins, if she loses one coin, does not light a lamp, sweep the house, and search carefully until she finds it? Luke 15:8

According to Jesus the third master key for recovering the "lost tenth coin" is "searching carefully." What does this expression mean? Search carefully means that if the church wants to restore the lost tenth coin, it must start by forensically investigating why it lost "tenth coin" in the first place. This is what happened to me over two decades ago, when I was confronted by a very sincere and godly child of God who told me plainly, "Why is not my tithing working for me? The windows of heaven I was promised by my pastors have never opened for me. What I am doing wrong?" These sincere tear-drenched questions arrested me in my track. I knew instantly that I could not answer her sincere tithing questions at the same level they were created at. This led me into "years" on intensive biblical research on this vital subject. This went on until the Holy Spirit divinely intercepted me in the fourteenth chapter of Genesis. For the first time, I saw and discovered the "priesthood" of Melchizedek.

❧❧❧❧❧
**The tithe (tenth coin) is never lost in the marketplace;
it is always lost among the body of believers.**
❧❧❧❧❧

By "searching carefully," I discovered that the tithing system that is New Testament compliant is "Tithing under the Order of Melchizedek." I discovered that Abraham never tithed for money because he already had lots of money before the LORD introduced him to the Kingdom principle of tithing. I discovered that Melchizedek is the first priest ever mentioned in Scripture, which means that the priesthood of all believers is not Levitical but of that order. I discovered that Abraham tithed for divine interception and for inclusion into the priesthood of Melchizedek. *Tithing into Melchizedek meant that Abraham had officially accepted here on earth Melchizedek's heavenly priesthood.* I discovered that Abram's act of partaking of communion and giving of "tithes" official initiated him into Melchizedek's eternal priesthood. Its no wonder Abraham became the father of many nations. He was the first human to officially enter into the priesthood of Melchizedek through the vehicle of tithing!

Until She Finds It!

"Or what woman, having ten silver coins, if she loses one coin, does not light a lamp, sweep the house, and search carefully until she finds it? Luke 15:8

According to Jesus the fourth and final key for recovering the "lost tenth coin" is "until she finds it!" What does this expression mean? This expression underscores the "spirit of determination" that Jesus expects the church to possess in order to "restore the lost art of tithing." If tithing was simply about bringing money into the coffers of the church, why would Jesus who "did not highly esteem" money, use such an expression? It is because the "Kingdom principle of tithing" is not about money. It's really about God's eternal genius. God knows that left to ourselves in a world that "worships money" we would also be hardcore worshippers at the altar of mammon. So God devised a "righteous trading platform" (tithing) on which God lets us exchange "carnal/material things" (money) in order to "access" what "money cannot buy" (true riches). Listen to how Paul the apostle describes this principle or trading platform. 1 Corinthians 9:11, "If we have sown spiritual things for you, is it a great thing if we reap your material things?"

Essentially "tithing" which is the highest form of giving in the entire bible is recognition that someone (a priest/pastor) who has sown into your life "spiritual things" is duly authorized by God to collect your "material things" (money). However, once your "priest/pastor" collects your "material things" God moves in to "seal" in your life the "spiritual things" that have been "sown in your heart." What a divine exchange! I am convinced after many years of critical observation that the main reason "the Word of God" fails to transform or stick to many churchgoers is due to the lack of tithing. Let me ask you a question. If I told you that every time you give me a $1 bill, I will give you a $100 bill, "how many times would you trade me for it?" I believe the answer is a no-brainer. This is exactly what tithing is about. *Tithing is about trading the "infinitely less valuable" (money) for the "infinitely priceless" (true riches).* How many times would you be involved in such a trade? I rest my case.

❧❧❧❧❧❧

Tithing into Melchizedek meant that
Abraham had officially accepted here on earth
Melchizedek's heavenly priesthood.

❧❧❧❧❧❧

The Fruit of Recovery

And when she has found it, she calls her friends and neighbors together, saying, 'Rejoice with me, for I have found the piece which I lost!' [10] *Likewise, I say to you, there is joy in the presence of the angels of God over one sinner who repents." Luke 15:9-10*

Jesus finally gets to the main reason He took time to tell this very important parable. Jesus shows us in the story the "fruit" that comes out of the "recovery of the lost tenth coin." When the woman (the local church) found the lost "tenth coin," she started rejoicing. She first called her "friends." Who are the "friends" in the parable? The "friends" are the ones who are the first beneficiaries of what the woman does with the "lost tenth coin." So it's safe to say the "friends" are members of the local church who are the first beneficiaries of what "tithes" do for any church. "Tithes" pay for the lights in the church, so I don't have to read the Bible in the dark when I attend church. Tithes pay for the church's full-time staff, who help the pastor make sure that all members of the church (including me) are taken care of. Tithes paid for the nice church music instruments and video presentations that help to richly enhance my worship experience. Tithes helps to pay for the cookies and snacks that the children's church buys to feed my children in children's church. The list goes on. So the "loss of the tenth coin" for any church is no small matter.

Secondly, She first called her "neighbors." Who are the "neighbors" in the parable? The "neighbors" are the ones who are the second beneficiaries of what the woman does with the "lost tenth coin." So its safe to say the ""neighbors"" represents the church's outreach to the local community where the church is domiciled in. The church's "neighbors" are widows, orphans, troubled teens in the community, prisoners, prostitutes, and the list can go on. I can tell you from experience that a church without money for these community outreach programs is useless to the local community. It might as well not even exist. When I speak with Pastors who are outreach minded, this is their biggest frustration and burden. They want to help the widows and orphans, but the lack of tithing has them arrested in a perpetual survival mode, barely keeping the doors of their church open. Its no wonder, Satan loves to attack "tithing." Unfortunately, so many so-called bible-believing Christians are helping the devil massacre the church in this area. Look at Europe the church is hanging on a single thread. What used to be beautiful Christ professing churches are now "taverns" serving hardcore liquor to a population on an express highway to hell! God help us, in Jesus name!!!

Finally, Jesus gets to the most critical part of the parable of the "lost tenth coin." "Likewise, I say to you, there is joy in the presence of the angels of God over one sinner who repents." What is here talking about? I though this parable was about the "lost tenth coin." What has story got to do with His last statement? Jesus is telling us that just as the economy of the local church runs on finding the "lost tenth coin;" "lost sinners" turning to Christ fuel heavens' economy. Jesus takes us behind the veil to show us that heaven throws a party every time a sinner on earth turns to Christ. However, the job of converting sinners "the lost" to Christ is the number one duty of the "Woman (local church)" in the parable.

❧❧❧❧❧❧❧

Tithing is about trading the "infinitely less valuable"
(money) for the "infinitely priceless" (true riches).

❧❧❧❧❧❧❧

However, the "Woman (local church)" cannot do much in her efforts to win the lost to Christ, if she is in permanent "survival mode" financially speaking. Billy Graham brought many souls to Christ and yet his outreaches cost the Billy Graham Evangelist Association millions of dollars. How could he have done it, if his ministry was penniless? So what is the moral of the parable of the lost tenth coin? It is simply this, "without the fuel of the tenth coin in the engines of the church's evangelism, reaching the lost for Christ becomes seriously compromised." Child of God asks yourself this question: "Do you really need money that much, that you are willing to destroy the church's ability to evangelize the lost for Christ by withholding your "tithes of honor" that rightfully belongs to the LORD?" **I rest my case.**

LIFE APPLICATION SECTION

Point to Ponder:

Tithing is the primary financing mechanism God set in place for the house of God (church) in order to advance the Kingdom of God.

Memory Verse:

"Or what woman, having ten silver coins, if she loses one coin, does not light a lamp, sweep the house, and search carefully until she finds it? Luke 15:8

Questions to Consider:

1. What is the significance of the coin that the woman lost in the parable?

_____
_____
_____
_____

2. List down two things the woman in the parable of the lost coin di to restore the lost coin.

_____
_____
_____
_____

3. What Jesus says happens in heaven when one sinner repents?

_____
_____
_____
_____

Chapter Twelve

Prophetic Significance of the Number 10

And blessed be God Most High, who has defeated your enemies for you." Then Abram gave Melchizedek a tenth of all the goods he had recovered. Genesis 14:20 (NLT)

T**hey are those** who say that God doesn't really care about numbers. Consequently, it does not really matter how much you give, provided it comes from your heart. At face value, their thinking seems justified. However, nothing could be further from the truth. A God who goes out of His way to author a book called "Numbers" understands that numbers do matter. People who are familiar with the Hebrew language, in which, the Bible was written in; know that Hebrew is one of the richest languages on Earth. Many biblical scholars believe that God created the Hebrew language to communicate His mind. In the Hebrew language "words or letters" correspond to a "number or set of numbers." Consequently, in Hebrew, a "number or set of numbers" can lead to "words or letters" in the Hebrew alphabet. This is why translating the bible from Hebrew to English presented quite a challenge for translators because the Hebrew language is richer than the English language.

Consequently some "words or Hebrew concepts" are lost in translation. Have you ever wondered why God inspired Abraham to give a "tenth of everything" he had obtained in battle? Why not 15%,

40% or even 100%? What is the prophetic significance of the number 10 in the Hebrew language? Before we dive into answering this question as it relates to the mystery of the tithe, I want you to read an article on the prophetic significance of the number 10 by Elizabeth A. Nixon, Esq.

"A little online research and I discovered why the number 10 is said to represent Perfection of Divine Order. Under our decimal number system, the number 10 is both the beginning of a new order of numbers and is the culmination of the numbers that come before it. But this is not unique to our modern numbering system. The ancient alphabet and numeric systems in Hebrew and Greek, which systems and principles are incorporated into the Bible, use the same numbering system based on 10.

For example, the number values assigned to the Hebrew and Greek letters show a numbering system where values are given from one to ten, then increasing in tens to 100, then increasing by 100's and so on. Of interest is the anatomical connection where the number 10 is the perfect number, i.e.: ten fingers and ten toes. Since ancient times, the number 10 has meant completeness of order, meaning that nothing is lacking and nothing is left over. It signifies that the cycle is complete and everything is in its proper order.

This is why the number 10 is said to represent Perfection of Divine Order. Then just yesterday, rather randomly, I found myself reading: John 10:10 which says: "The thief comes only to steal, kill and destroy; I [Jesus] have come that they might have life and might have it more abundantly." Could it be that the significance of all the tens is that we are in a month (or season) where we can enter into the Perfection of Divine Order for our lives? 10:10 presents us with a choice: a life stolen, killed and destroyed by the thief, or an abundant life found in Jesus Christ. (A Prophetic Word about 10:10 by Elizabeth A. Nixon, Esq.)

≪୨∘୨∘≪୨∘୨

The number 10 is said to represent Perfection of Divine Order.

≪୨∘୨∘≪୨∘୨

Prophetic Numerology

In the school of prophecy, "prophetic numerology' is the study of numbers that are prophetically significant to the interpretation of biblical events and concepts. For instance:

(i.)   The number 50 corresponds to the year of Jubilee, which is the fiftieth year on the Jewish calendar, which is a month of emancipation from every kind of bondage. In the year of Jubilee, everybody who was in debt was released. "In addition, you must count off seven Sabbath years, seven sets of seven years, adding up to forty-nine years in all. Then on the Day of Atonement in the fiftieth year,[a] blow the ram's horn loud and long throughout the land. 10 Set this year apart as holy, a time to proclaim freedom throughout the land for all who live there. It will be a jubilee year for you, when each of you may return to the land that belonged to your ancestors and return to your own clan." Leviticus 25: 8-10 (NLT)

(ii.) The number 1 corresponds with "God's eternal oneness or the union between husband and wife." "Hear, O Israel: The Lord our God, the Lord is one! You shall love the Lord your God with all your heart, with all your soul, and with all your strength. Deuteronomy 6:4-5

(iii.) The number 12 corresponds with "God's perfect government." This explains why God built Israel as nation of twelve tribes and Jesus chose twelve disciples. "Now it came to pass in those days that He went out to the mountain to pray, and continued all night in prayer to God. And when it was day, He called His disciples to Himself; and from them, He chose twelve whom He also named apostles:" Luke 6:12-13

(iv.) The number 3 corresponds with the eternal holy trinity or Godhead, and it is also the number of an unbreakable witness. "For there are three that bear witness in heaven: the Father, the Word, and the Holy Spirit; and these three are one." 1 John 5:7

(v.) The number 7 corresponds with "completeness, a finished process or a time of rest." "Thus the heavens and the earth, and all the host of them, were finished. 2 And on the seventh day, God ended His work, which He had done, and He rested on the seventh day from all His work, which He had done. Then God blessed the seventh day and sanctified it, because in it He rested from all His work which God had created and made." Genesis 2:1-3

It is not my intention to do an exhaustive discourse on biblical or prophetic numerology. I just wanted to make a point that Abraham giving a tenth to Melchizedek was not accidental. The fingerprint of God was all over it.

❧❧❧❧❧❧❧

In the year of Jubilee, everybody who was in debt was released.

❧❧❧❧❧❧❧

Perfect Divine Order

For God is not a God of disorder but of peace, as in all the meetings of God's holy people. 1 Corinthians 14:33 (NLT)

According to Elizabeth A. Nixon, the number values assigned to the Hebrew and Greek letters show a numbering system where values are given from one to ten, then increasing in tens to 100, then increasing by 100's and so on. Of interest is the anatomical connection where the number 10 is the perfect number, ie: ten fingers and ten toes. Since ancient times, the number 10 has meant completeness of order, meaning that nothing is lacking and nothing is left over. It signifies that the cycle is complete and everything is in its proper order. This is why the number 10 is said to represent Perfection of Divine Order.

It would not be far-fetched based upon the Hebrew language to say that when Abram gave Melchizedek a "tenth" of everything he had, Abraham's entire life came under "perfect divine order." Everything about him that was misaligned with the calendar of heaven was quickly synchronized by this one act of faith and worship. It's informative for us to realize that God did not commit to making Abraham the father of many nations until after his glorious encounter with the priesthood of Melchizedek. It goes without saying that when God's children give their "tithes of honor" willingly and from a joyful heart, they give the Holy Spirit permission to bring into divine order everything in their life that is out of alignment with the agenda of heaven.

A Time of Testing

These trials will show that your faith is genuine. It is being tested as fire tests and purifies gold—though your faith is far more precious than mere gold. So when your faith remains strong through many trials, it will bring you much praise and glory and honor on the day when Jesus Christ is revealed to the whole world. 1 Peter 1:7 (NLT)

In the Hebrew language, the number 10 also corresponds to the word "testing." This means that when God inspired Abram to give Him a tenth of everything he had, God was "testing" him for a higher assignment. We all know from going to school that a school "test" is always about "something higher." Every high school student knows that when they pass a "test or final exam" their reward will be admission to college. Colleges, especially prestigious Ivy League universities have high passing marks that they must be met before admission into their college. Failing the test means, "forfeiting the higher thing!"

Tithing is God testing us with "materials things" to see if we are qualified to be entrusted with true riches. Listen carefully to what Jesus says in Luke 16:11 (NLT), "And if you are untrustworthy about worldly wealth, who will trust you with the true riches of heaven?" The spiritual implications of Jesus' statement is staggering. The phrase "Who will trust you" is another way of Jesus saying, "Not Me!" In other words, if you cannot be trusted to honor God with a "tenth" of your worldly wealth, how can God entrust the true riches of heaven into your hands? Can I submit to you that every time you are faithful in the giving of your "tithes" you are "setting yourself up" for the "something higher" that God has in store for you.

❧❧❧❧❧❧❧

*Tithing is God testing us with "materials things"
to see if we are qualified to be entrusted with true riches.*

❧❧❧❧❧❧❧

LIFE APPLICATION SECTION

Point to Ponder:

The number ten is an important number in biblical numerology, representing perfect divine order and alignment.

Memory Verse:

For God is not a God of disorder but of peace, as in all the meetings of God's holy people. 1 Corinthians 14:33 (NLT)

Questions to Consider:

1. What else does the number 10 represent in biblical numeric?

_____

_____

_____

_____

2. Is tithing another way God uses to test our stewardship here on earth?

_____

_____

_____

_____

3. How did God test Abraham on Mount Moriah?

_____

_____

_____

_____

Chapter Thirteen

The Power of the Tithe

Here mortal men receive tithes, but there he receives them, of whom it is witnessed that he lives. ⁹ Even Levi, who receives tithes, paid tithes through Abraham, so to speak, ¹⁰ for he was still in the loins of his father when Melchizedek met him. Hebrews 7:8-9

The "Power of the Tithe" between the Levitical priestly order and the Order of Melchizedek is significantly different. Comparing the "power of the tithe" under these two divine priestly orders is like comparing the power of a grenade to the power of a nuclear bomb. If you were to drop a grenade in a crowded market, you might kill and injure a handful of people and cause a little bit of structural damage. On the other hand, if we were to drop a nuclear bomb, the resulting loss of lives and the ensuing structural damage would be catastrophic.

I know that this illustration might be too graphic for some people, but I am trying to illustrate the astronomical difference between the power of the tithe under the priestly order of Aaron and the priestly order of Melchizedek. There are seven major factors, which determine the power of the tithe that we will examine closely in this chapter. Just bear in mind that there is "no tithe," which is higher than the priestly order it serves. Every tithe leads you to the priesthood it services and makes the "tither" a beneficiary of the spirit dynamics the priesthood offers.

The Nature of the High Priest

The first spiritual factor, which affects the "power of the tithe," is the "spiritual nature of the High Priest who presides over the priesthood" that we are tithing into. Consider for instance that Eli's tenure as the High Priest over the nation of Israel released spiritual darkness and apathy in the nation because of his spiritual passivity. When Samuel was about twelve years old when the Word of the Lord came to him. The first book of Samuel describes in great detail the prevailing spiritual atmosphere at the time with this expression: "the visions of God were rare in those days." When the presiding priesthood is corrupt and weak in its spiritual dynamics, the "proceeding Word of God becomes rare, and the light of God's Word fails to shine brightly."

> *"Meanwhile, the boy Samuel served the Lord by assisting Eli. Now in those days messages from the Lord were very rare, and visions were quite uncommon. [2] One night Eli, who was almost blind by now, had gone to bed. [3] The lamp of God had not yet gone out, and Samuel was sleeping in the Tabernacle near the Ark of God."*
> 1 Samuel 3:1-2

Every priesthood draws its life and anointing from the spiritual stature of its High Priest. This is why Eli's failure to father and discipline his sons, Hophni and Phinehas, short-circuited the flow and move of God in the priesthood of Eli. God failed to do mighty things through the priesthood of Eli because his "passivity as a natural father" to his sons had seriously compromised the spiritual integrity of his priesthood. The priesthood lost its spiritual potency and became set on the pathway of death. Under Eli's watch, the ungodly Philistines "captured the Ark of God!"

Comparing the "power of the tithe" under
these two divine priestly orders is like comparing
the power of a grenade to the power of a nuclear bomb.

When Eli heard of this, he fell from his chair, broke his neck and died. Aaron, the first High Priest of the nation of Israel, was also subject to "demonic influences and human manipulation." When the people of Israel saw that Moses was taking too long in returning to them from his time with God, they "pressured Aaron to make them a golden calf which they could worship in place of God!" Aaron succumbed to the constant pressure from the people and made them a diabolical golden calf that they started worshipping. This diabolical action by Aaron, who was the presiding High Priest at the time, opened the door for spiritual invasion by demon-powers and compromised the power and integrity of the priesthood.

> *"All the people took the gold rings from their ears and brought them to Aaron. Then Aaron took the gold, melted it down, and molded it into the shape of a calf. When the people saw it, they exclaimed, 'O Israel, these are the gods who brought you out of the land of Egypt!'"* Exodus 32:3-4

Under the priestly Order of Melchizedek, our High Priest is both the "perfect man and God Almighty." Jesus Christ was so much man that He got hungry and also got tired. He was so much God that when He spoke to a man who had been dead for four days, He raised him from the dead. His spiritual nature is one of complete and uninterrupted righteousness. The high priest of the priestly Order of Melchizedek has never been stained by personal sin. He lives in a place of mastery over the machinery of sin and death. He is the very essence of the anointing. He is the "Christ" which literally means, "the anointed One and His anointing." No other High Priest has ever worn this title.

Even though all the High Priests under the Levitical priesthood were anointed by God, none of them was "saturated with the presence and anointing of the Holy Spirit" like Jesus was. The testimony of the Prophet John the Baptist concerning the High Priest (Jesus Christ) of the priestly Order of Melchizedek is simply this; "...to Him has been given the Spirit without measure" (John 2). We can't even fathom the unlimited measure of spiritual power, which the High Priest of the priestly Order of Melchizedek brings to bear upon the "tithe of those who tithe into His eternal priestly Order." The "Malachi 3:8-12 tithing model" connects our tithe to the "limited anointing and spiritual stature" of the earth-bound priesthood of Levi. When we employ the Malachi tithing system, we are short-circuiting and limiting our own spiritual blessings.

"The law appointed high priests who were limited by human weakness. But after the law was given, God appointed his Son with an oath, and his Son has been made the perfect High Priest forever."
Hebrews 7:28

Every priesthood draws its life and anointing from the spiritual stature of its High Priest.

The Spiritual Rank of the High Priest

The second critical factor, which seriously affects the power of the tithe between the Levitical priesthood and the Order of Melchizedek, is "the spiritual rank of the presiding High Priest." Everything in the Kingdom of God and in the kingdom of darkness is based upon spiritual ranking. The spiritual rank a person occupies within the eternal structures of the Kingdom of Heaven will greatly influence how demon-powers and circumstances respond to the sound of their voice of command. Let's consider for a moment the role which spiritual ranking played in the humiliation of the seven sons of Sceva who were overpowered by a demon-possessed man.

A group of Jews was traveling from town to town casting out evil spirits. They tried to use the name of the Lord Jesus in their exorcism, saying, "I command you in the name of Jesus, whom Paul preaches, to come out!" Seven sons of Sceva, a leading priest, were doing this. But one time when they tried it, the evil spirit replied, "I

know Jesus, and I know Paul, but who are you?" Then the man with
the evil spirit leaped on them, overpowered them, and attacked them
with such violence that they fled from the house, naked and battered.
Acts 19:13-16

The seven sons of Sceva observed the apostle Paul casting out demons and sought to imitate him. They thought that Paul's spiritual power and authority over demonic spirits was derived from a spiritual formula. So they copied Paul's method for casting out demons and tried to duplicate this spiritual technology with disastrous consequences. They went into the house of a demon-possessed man and began the process of casting out the evil spirits that were residing in him. Here is what they said to the demon-powers: "We charge you to come out of this man in the name of Jesus Christ whom Paul preaches about!"

At the sound of their voice of command, the demon-possessed man responded by saying, "Jesus we know and Paul we know, but who are you?" The demonic spirits inside this man knew that the sons of Sceva had no spiritual rank of authority in the realm of the spirit. What followed spread like wildfire throughout the City of Ephesus and brought the whole City under the fear of the Lord. The demon-possessed man rose and overpowered the seven sons of Sceva and beat them naked. They ran into the City streets naked and bleeding profusely.

But to the Son, he says, "Your throne, O God, endures forever and
ever. You rule with a scepter of justice." Hebrews 1:8

The "spiritual rank" of the High Priest of the Order of Melchizedek is one of the "loftiest spiritual ranks ever held by a man." First and foremost under the Order of Melchizedek, our High Priest is God Most High. The High Priest of the New Testament Order of Melchizedek priesthood is as "divine and as eternal as God the Father." He (Christ) has no beginning of days or end of life. Everything in creation was created by Him and through Him. This in itself places Him in spiritual rank, which no other man could ever attain to. We know for a fact that the High Priests of the Levitical priesthood were "mere mortals chosen from among men."

150

They had a spiritual rank that was based upon the office of the high priest, which God gave them under the Mosaic Covenant.

> *"Therefore, God elevated him to the place of highest honor and gave him the name above all other names, that at the name of Jesus every knee should bow, in heaven and on earth and under the earth."*
> Philippians 2:9-10

Secondly, as the High Priest of the Order of Melchizedek, Jesus also occupies the "loftiest spiritual position the heavenly Father has ever given to a man!" The apostle Paul shows us from the above passage of Scripture how Jesus earned this lofty position. Saint Paul tells us that Jesus' life of total obedience to God, even to the point of sacrificing His own life by embracing the shameful death of the cross "earned Him this lofty position of authority." The apostle Paul tells us that because of His life of explicit obedience to God, that God gave Him (Jesus) a name that is above every other name.

This name has "complete authority in heaven, on earth, and in the underworld!" The usage of the word "name" in this passage literally means "title." When a heavyweight boxer defeats every opponent in his division, he is given the title of world heavyweight boxing champion. This new title describes the fact that, the said boxer holds the loftiest rank in the whole world of boxing. Jesus completely defeated sin, the devil and death and as such God gave Him the loftiest title ever given to a man and then set Him on the right hand of the throne of God.

This is why tithing into the priestly Order of Melchizedek is so very powerful. The lofty spiritual rank of its High Priest "multiplies the spiritual power backing our tithe," compared to tithing into the Levitical priesthood. When we tithe as Abraham tithed we "increase the power of our tithe exponentially!" This would explain why the devil would love to see the global Church continue to employ the Malachi 3:8-12 tithing system.

The Spiritual Authority of the High Priest

Jesus came and told his disciples, "I have been given all authority in heaven and on earth. Therefore, go and make disciples of all the nations, baptizing them in the name of the Father and the Son and the Holy Spirit. Teach these new disciples to obey all the commands I have given you. And be sure of this: I am with you always, even to the end of the age." Matthew 28:18-20

The third spiritual factor, which affects the power of the tithe between the Levitical priesthood and the Order of Melchizedek, is the "spiritual authority of the High Priest." Let us examine the level of spiritual authority that God invested in the High Priests of the Levitical priesthood and then compare their level of spiritual authority to that of the High Priest of the priestly Order of Melchizedek. The High Priest of the Levitical priesthood had a very "limited scope of spiritual authority." First and foremost their spiritual authority was limited to "governing the daily affairs of the temple and meeting the spiritual needs of the Jewish nation." The high priest under the Levitical priesthood had dismal spiritual authority over the kings and prophets of Israel, who were given a different anointing and function within the nation of Israel.

"Therefore, God elevated him to the place of highest honor and gave him the name above all other names, that at the name of Jesus every knee should bow, in heaven and on earth and under the earth." Philippians 2:9-10

On the other hand, the High Priest of the Order of Melchizedek has an "unlimited scope of spiritual authority." His spiritual authority is deep and far-reaching. When Jesus rose from the dead, He told His apprentice apostles that they could go into the entire world in the power of His name, because He had been given "all authority in heaven and on earth!" The apostle Paul also tells us that Jesus Christ, the High Priest of the Order of Melchizedek, was given a "name higher than any other name." This name yields tremendous spiritual authority in the spirit world. The

Bible says that at the mention of this name, "every knee in heaven, on earth and in the underworld has to bow and confess" that Jesus Christ is Lord. What an authority!

✧✧✧✧✧✧✧

As the High Priest of the Order of Melchizedek,
Jesus also occupies the "loftiest spiritual position
the heavenly Father has ever given to a man!"

✧✧✧✧✧✧✧

It is safe to assume that when we tithe into the Order of Melchizedek, the "highest form of spiritual authority known to man and angels is superimposed over our tithes." The unlimited scope of authority of the High priest of the Order of Melchizedek gives our tithe the spiritual authority and power to release whatever belongs to us, whether those things are being held up in heaven or on earth. The tithe also gains the power to release whatever is being held up by demonic powers from the underworld. Since the spiritual authority of the High Priest of the Order of Melchizedek extends to every known spiritual and natural border, our tithe also takes on this power. This means that tithing into the Order of Melchizedek can open up entire nations for Kingdom advancement.

The Spiritual Scope of the Tithe

"Here is the main point: We have a High Priest who sat down in the place of honor beside the throne of the majestic God in heaven. There he ministers in the heavenly Tabernacle, the true place of worship that was built by the Lord and not by human hands." Hebrews 8:1-2

The fourth spiritual factor, which affects the power of the tithe between the Levitical priesthood and the priestly Order of Melchizedek, is the "spiritual scope of the tithe." When we talk about the spiritual scope of the tithe we are talking about the size of the spiritual territory the tithe covers. The spiritual scope of the tithe is tied to the spiritual scope of the priesthood it serves. We know that the Levitical priesthood was an earthly priesthood based upon the "shadow of things to come" and that its spiritual reach did not extend beyond the borders of the nation of Israel. This is why the Levitical tithe could only open the "windows of heaven" because it serviced an earthly priesthood, which was "operating from the outside of the true sanctuary which is in heaven." The Malachi 3:8-12 tithing system is limited to opening the windows of heaven, but it has "no power to open the doors of the Kingdom of heaven." To open the doors of heaven would require that one possesses the "keys of the kingdom of heaven," which this priesthood did not have access to.

"Bring all the tithes into the storehouse so there will be enough food in my Temple. If you do," says the Lord of Heaven's Armies, "I will open the windows of heaven for you. I will pour out a blessing so great you won't have enough room to take it in! Try it! Put me to the test!" Malachi 3:10

On the other hand, the "spiritual scope" of the tithe that is based upon the Abrahamic tithing system is "vast and far-reaching." This is because this Abrahamic tithing system serves a priesthood, which "operates from the inside of the heavenly temple." This is why this tithing system can open the doors of the kingdom of Heaven because the tithers (New Covenant believers) have been given the "keys of the kingdom of Heaven." This is why it saddens me when I hear well-meaning teachers of the gospel tell New Testament believers that when they tithe, God will open the windows of heaven. "Please remember that if we are being fed through windows, then we are still living and operating from the outside of the Father's house!"

"And I will give you the keys of the Kingdom of Heaven. Whatever you forbid on earth will be forbidden in heaven, and whatever you permit on earth will be permitted in heaven." Matthew 16:19

The Ministry of the High Priest

"But now Jesus, our High Priest, has been given a ministry that is far superior to the old priesthood, for he is the one who mediates for us a far better covenant with God, based on better promises."
Hebrews 8:6

The fifth spiritual factor, which differentiates the power of the tithe between the Levitical priesthood and the Order of Melchizedek, is "the spiritual ministry" of the High Priest. The apostle Paul tells us that Christ's superiority over the High Priests of the Levitical priesthood is also based upon the fact that Jesus has a more "excellent ministry than they did" which is "established upon a superior covenant." The apostle Paul calls this excellent ministry the "ministry of the Spirit," whereas the ministry of the High Priests of the Levitical priesthood was the "ministry of the letter." In the entire Old Testament, you will not find any High Priest under the Levitical priesthood who had a ministry of "raising the dead, casting out devils and healing the sick." Yet we see the High Priest of the Order of Melchizedek, our Lord Jesus Christ, operating in "all of these dimensions of the Spirit." This means that when we tithe into the Order of Melchizedek, our tithe "literally activates God's resurrection and healing power over our lives."

The Covenant the Priesthood Stands On!

"But now Jesus, our High Priest, has been given a ministry that is far superior to the old priesthood, for he is the one who mediates for us a far better covenant with God, based on better promises."
Hebrews 8:6

The sixth spiritual factor, which determines the power of the tithe, is the "covenant that the priesthood stands on." Please remember that there is "no tithing system" that is not attached to" priesthood." Tithing is always tied to exclusively to priesthood. The apostle Paul tells us that the Order of Melchizedek of which our Lord Jesus is the presiding High

Priest is superior to the Levitical priesthood because it is "established on a more excellent covenant with God!" This covenant comes packaged with "excellent promises" for the people who live under this royal priesthood. This is why tithing into the Order of Melchizedek can activate the manifestation of precious promises of God from His holy Word. There are many of God's people who are "nursing unfulfilled personal prophecies." I truly believe that when we begin to tithe into the Order of Melchizedek, God will "supernaturally quicken the fulfillment" of prophetic promises He has given us in the past, just as He did for Abraham when Melchizedek met him.

The Primary Motivation Behind the Tithe

Behold I have given the children of Levi all the tithes in Israel as an Inheritance in return for the work which they perform, the work of the tabernacle of meeting. Numbers 18:21

Tithing under the Levitical priesthood was no different than dining at a good restaurant and then refusing to pay for the meal. This act would be called "stealing from the owner of the restaurant." This is the contextual application of Malachi 3:8-12.

The primary motivation for the Malachi 3:8-12 pattern of tithing is "payment for priestly services." This would explain why New Testament believers who use Malachi 3:8-12 as a tithing model have an "inherent expectation of service" from their pastors when they "pay" their tithes. This would explain why some Christians get very angry and vindictive when they feel that their pastors are not giving them sufficient pastoral care. God help the pastor who fails to visit them in person when they are sick. Many of these Christians choose to hold the local Church hostage by withholding their tithes.

The first station of their outraged will is evidenced in the "withholding of their tithes" from their local Church. Many of these Christians conclude that their senior pastor forfeited his or her ability to command their "tithe" when he or she failed to provide the necessary priestly services that they felt they were entitled to. If the senior pastor does not play to their tune, they leave the church immediately. They leave the Church and start searching for a new Church where they can find a pastor who is willing to work very hard at earning their tithe. Many good churches have been destroyed by this "demonic mentality and culture" because our "tithing model as we have taught it, is fundamentally flawed."

ৰ৶৾৾ঌ৾ৰ৶৾৾ঌ৾

Jesus has a more "excellent ministry than they did"
which is "established upon a superior covenant."

ৰ৶৾৾ঌ৾ৰ৶৾৾ঌ৾

Under the priestly Order of Melchizedek, the "giving of tithe" has nothing to do with "paying for priestly services rendered." Under this eternal priestly Order, God expects us to "give our tithes" whether we get the necessary priestly services from our pastors or not. Under this divine priestly Order, we cannot exercise the option of withholding our tithes in an effort to punish the "senior pastor or hold the local Church hostage." *Tithing under the priestly Order of Melchizedek is not "payment for services rendered, but a royal endowment" bestowed on His royal majesty by His "Kingdom citizens" for the "continued privilege" of working on the "King's land."* When the global Church comes into this "prevailing Kingdom mentality" of tithing, we will see the "Day of God" breakout in the church and marketplace.

The Functions and Features of the Tithe

Here mortal men receive tithes, but there he receives them, of whom
it is witnessed that he lives. [9] Even Levi, who receives tithes, paid
tithes through Abraham, so to speak, Hebrews 7:8-9

The final spiritual factor, which determines the power of the tithe under these two priestly orders is the "distinctive functions and features" of the tithe. These distinctive functions and features allude to the power that God has invested in the tithe. We will now quickly examine these distinctive features and functions. The "tithe" under the Levitical priesthood was a payment for priestly services rendered, whereas, under the Order of Melchizedek, the "tithe" is given as a royal endowment to honor the "King" (Christ) and extend His "Kingdom" here on earth.

Under the Order of Melchizedek, the "tithe" is given to express heartfelt honor for His Majesty King Jesus, our eternal High Priest, whereas under the Levitical priesthood, the "tithe" was given out of a sense of legal obligation. The "tithe" under the Levitical priesthood was a "transitional tithe" which was designed to service the Jewish nation until the installation of Christ's New Testament Order of Melchizedek priesthood. Under the Melchizedek priesthood, the "tithes" of Kingdom citizens are used to support and sustain the advancement of the Kingdom of God here on earth, whereas under the Levitical priestly order the "tithes" of the Jewish nation were used primarily to support and sustain the priesthood.

Under the Levitical priesthood, non-tithers were punished by a "curse" as prescribed by the Law of Moses. Under the priestly Order of Melchizedek, non-tithers are chastised with a diminished capacity for manifesting the FAVOR of God! Under the New Testament of covenant of grace, instead of cursing non-tithers, God simply diminishes the level of favor or stewardship on their lives. How can God entrust us with true riches when we are not faithful with mammon.

LIFE APPLICATION SECTION

Point to Ponder:

The difference in the power of the tithe between the Levitical order and the order of Melchizedek is like comparing a grenade to a nuclear bomb.

Memory Verse:

"The law appointed high priests who were limited by human weakness. But after the law was given, God appointed his Son with an oath, and his Son has been made the perfect High Priest forever." Hebrews 7:28

Questions to Consider:

1. How does the fact that the priestly Order of Melchizedek is established on a better covenant affect the power of tithe?

_____

_____

_____

_____

2. What are the other spiritual factors that affect the power of the tithe?

_____

_____

_____

_____

3. How does the spiritual rank of the High priest affect the power of the tithe?

_____

_____

_____

_____

Epilogue

Activation: Suggested Tithing Prayer

Now it came to pass, as He was praying in a certain place, when He ceased, that one of His disciples said to Him, "Lord, teach us to pray, as John also taught his disciples." ² So He said to them, "When you pray, say: Our Father in heaven, Hallowed be Your name. Your kingdom come. Your will be done on earth as it is in heaven.
Luke 11:1-2

Perhaps there is no activity as lofty as "prayer" within the economy of the Kingdom. Almost every world religion on earth prays, some more regularly than others. However, the Lord Jesus shows us in the gospels that it's not just praying that is important. It's accurate praying that moves the hand of God. I have spent the whole book establishing a new and higher order of tithing in the body of Christ. For this reason it's important that after reading this book, tithing should take on a new whole meaning. This is why I have taken the liberty to craft a "Tithing Prayer" that can be used by both churches and individuals to ensure that they are tithing correctly. The tithing prayer below is New Testament compliant. There is no legalism in this prayer whatsoever. You will find that the spirit of grace is on this anointed prayer.

Tithing Prayer

"Heavenly Father, thank you that I am the New Creation in Christ Jesus and that I am also a member of the Order of Melchizedek under the headship of the Lord Jesus Christ, my royal High Priest. Heavenly Father, You have called me to be a king and a priest in the Earth. I come boldly before your Throne of Grace through the blood of Jesus to offer sacrifices of praise and adoration. Heavenly Father, You are the King of the Universe and my creator, and as such you are worthy of all my adoration and honor. I bring my "tithes of honor" to your throne room in a spirit of heartfelt humility and honor.

Lord Jesus, I am tithing not because I am afraid that you might Curse me if I do not tithe. I am already blessed with every spiritual blessing in Christ Jesus according to Ephesians 1:3. I am tithing to acknowledge your Lordship over my life and property. I tithe to excite the supernatural release of the heavenly bread and wine that I need to achieve my destiny. I tithe because I know that my tithes shall be used to advance your Kingdom on the earth and I love your Kingdom.

Precious Holy Spirit, I am also tithing to activate the technology of divine interception in my life. I decree and declare that God will always get to me before the death and his wicked devices can get to me or take me out. Heavenly Father, I am also tithing to shut down the engines of greed in my life and ministry. I am also tithing to demonstrate that I am a faithful steward of the mysteries of God.

Heavenly Father, I am tithing to overturn and overthrow the train of the king of Sodom that is headed my way. Lord, I am also tithing to sanctify all the channels of wealth creation in my life. Lord take the spirit of mammon out of my life and finances. For it is written the blessing of the Lord makes rich and He adds no sorrow to it. I am tithing to confirm the covenant of faith that God made with my father, Abraham. Holy Spirit, I am also tithing to activate my God-given, infinite imagination for multibillion-dollar business ideas and witty inventions. Heavenly Father, I am not tithing for money, but I know that when I tithe correctly, you will make sure that money will always attend to my life. For the destruction of the poor is their poverty. I am not poor, and I will never live in poverty, for Christ became poor that for His sake, I might be made rich. In Jesus name I pray. Amen

Made in the USA
Middletown, DE
10 November 2021